Published by Melbourne Books
Level 9, 100 Collins Street
Melbourne, VIC 3000
Australia
www.melbournebooks.com.au
info@melbournebooks.com.au

First Edition: September 2008
Second Edition: September 2009
Third Edition: October 2010
Fourth Edition: October 2011
Fifth Edition: November 2012
Sixth Edition: September 2013
Seventh Edition: October 2014
Eighth Edition: August 2015
Ninth Edition: August 2016
Tenth Edition: August 2017
Eleventh Edition: September 2018

Title: Award Winning Australian Writing 2018:
The best winning writing from short story and poetry
competitions nationally
Managing Editor: David Tenenbaum
Editors: Iryna Byelyayeva and Alexandra Milne
ISBN: 9781925556377

For information on how to be part of
Award Winning Australian Writing, visit
www.melbournebooks.com.au/awaw-submissions

Find us on Facebook at
www.facebook.com/AwardWinningAustralianWriting

This edition is available via print on demand or as ebook
through your preferred platform.

NATIONAL
LIBRARY
OF AUSTRALIA

A catalogue record for this
book is available from the
National Library of Australia

CONTENTS

5   **IRYNA BYELYAYEVA and ALEXANDRA MILNE**   INTRODUCTION

7   **JONATHAN O'BRIEN**   EVERY IDEA I HAD FOR MY AUSTRALIAN SHORT STORY
    COLLECTION
    State Library of Queensland Young Writers Award

11   **BRIANNA BULLEN**   A CONVERSATION BETWEEN EQUALS
    Apollo Bay Short Story Competition

15   **PENNY O'HARA**   THE THIRD DAUGHTER
    June Shenfield Poetry Award

16   **CATHERINE MAH**   THE POWER OF SNAILS
    2018 UTS Anthology Writing Prize

19   **FIKRET PAJALIC**   ALL THE WRONG THINGS
    Ada Cambridge Biographical prose Prize 2017

23   **KATELIN FARNSWORTH**   LOLLIES
    Verandah Genre Award 2017

27   **KAREN ANDREWS**   MIRIAM AND MILDRED
    2017 Alan Marshall Short Story Award (local division)

30   **KELLY SIMPSON**   VIEWPOINT
    *Stonnington Untitled Literary Festival open age
    category short story competition*

35   **ROGER VICKERY**   FLYING TO IPSWICH
    2017 Rolf Boldrewood Poetry Award

37   **RAFAEL S. W.**   A SHOEBOX NOT FILLED WITH SHOES
    City of Rockingham Short Fiction Awards 2017

43   **GUY SALVIDGE**   THE CENTRE CANNOT HOLD
    Joe O'Sullivan Writers' Prize

48	**MARK O'FLYNN**	KITE *Leon Shann Melbourne Poets Union International Poetry Award*
50	**KEVIN GILLAM**	FIGUE *Katherine Susannah Prichard Poetry Competition 2017*
52	**AVRIL BRADLEY**	FLIGHT OF THE MONARCHS *Poetica Christi Press. Theme: 'Wonderment'*
54	**MIRANDA TETLOW**	THIS IS WHERE YOU COME FROM *Northern Territory Literary Awards—ZipPrint Short Story Award*
60	**RACHAEL MEAD**	POWERLESS *2017 NALAG Grieve Poetry Prize*
61	**LAURA ELVERY**	UNSPOOLING *Neilma Sidney Short Story Prize*
66	**PAULETTE GITTINS**	ANOTHER GIG *2017 Trudy Graham/Julie Lewis Literary Award for Prose*
70	**KEVIN BONNETT**	COOL AND WET TO THE TOUCH *Cliff Green Short Story Competition*
72	**SHELLEY HANSEN**	MY NAME'S DOREEN *2017 Open Award & Marian Mayne Trophy, CJ Dennis Poetry Competition, Toolangi, Victoria*
75	**CASSIE HAMER**	IN THE DEEP *Shoalhaven Literary Award*
82		CONTRIBUTORS
86		COMPETITIONS

IRYNA BYELYAYEVA and ALEXANDRA MILNE
Editors

INTRODUCTION

A couple of months ago we were sitting at a bar with a group of fellow writers, when a friend placed their drink down and asked the big question: 'So, why do you write?'

Writing is responding. As writers, we crave the feeling of exploring our innermost feelings of love, loss, rejection, suffering and joy. Writers initiate important conversations and offer a view of life from a perspective that, perhaps, we otherwise wouldn't consider. As Australians, we are immensely lucky to be practicing our craft in this literary scene. With so many thought-provoking publications and inspiring competitions, our literary culture is thriving and every one of the pieces presented in this anthology adds another dimension to this landscape.

Award Winning Australian Writing is in its eleventh year. Once again, we had the pleasure of reading the best of the best of Australian writing. We opened each submission eagerly, keen to read the stories within. What surprised us most was the diversity of competitions won. We are proud that in this anthology

you will find winners from competitions run by major Melbourne journals, from rural poetry prizes and genre fiction competitions. There are submissions from all around Australia, about all aspects of life.

Some long-time readers may notice that this year you are holding a very different version of *AWAW*. As opposed to the classic book format, *AWAW* has transformed into a digital publication. It has always been the aim for *AWAW* to be the benchmark for aspiring writers and to ensure prize winners receive the attention their work deserves. Publishing emerging and established writers in this format is more accessible to a wider audience.

The most difficult aspect of editing *AWAW* is choosing what pieces to publish. How do you decide what entries are the best, when the prerequisite for submission is winning a national competition—to already be the best? We received so many wonderful pieces and attempted to choose a diverse range of plots, themes, mediums and writers. In *AWAW 2018* you will find writing about grief and loss, animals, adolescence, music and even creative writing groups. What we believe to be a special aspect of this year's anthology is how many of the stories are based on land and nature. Specifically, we felt as though there was a strong sense of Australiana that came through.

Because of the changed format of *AWAW,* we thought it was especially important to put careful thought into the structure of this year's publication. We began with Jonathan O'Brien's reflection on what many writers go through when they begin their creative process. A unique work of science fiction by Brianna Bullen reflects society today. 'Lollies', 'All the Wrong Things' and 'Miriam and Mildred' discuss serious topics with a lighter voice, moving on to pieces with a strong sense of the Australian landscape with 'Viewpoint' and 'A Shoebox not Filled with Shoes'.

It is inherent that, in fiction writing, people delve into the darker side of their selves. The mood of the anthology dips into themes of grief, loss and the power it takes from us. 'Unspooling' was the most recent winner of *Overland*'s fiction prize—a deeply emotional piece.

We wanted our readers to put down the anthology in a mood, not of sadness, but of introspection. 'Cool and Wet to the Touch' is a piece that is uplifting. 'In the Deep' will catch you by surprise and hopefully make you smile.

Throughout the anthology there are themes of animals, plants and how they can be used as motifs to reflect the broad spectrum of human emotions, from cows to seals to moths to figs. Long-form

pieces are interspersed with short poetry to break things up.

To answer the question posed to us six months ago at a sticky table over a glass of whiskey: we write for the same reason that we read—to live the lives that aren't our own, even for a short time. This anthology is unique because it invites you to its pages, both as a reader and as a writer. We hope that it's appreciated with this in mind and, from it, you take in something new, be it a perspective, a fun fact or simply a joyful reading experience.

We are grateful to all of our contributors for the wealth of material they gave us to choose from and to David Tenenbaum, the publisher here at Melbourne Books, for once again providing an avenue for writers to share their work, for the benefit of the literary landscape.

JONATHAN O'BRIEN
State Library of Queensland Young Writers Award

EVERY IDEA I HAD FOR MY AUSTRALIAN LITERATURE SHORT STORY COLLECTION

A divorced man seeks connection.

A divorced man drinks six tinnies on the back deck. He goes for a drive.

A divorced man goes to his son's cricket game. His son loses.

A divorced man calls his sister. She is preoccupied with a success he could never achieve.

A divorced man longs to work in agriculture, like all his friends. Out west, a storm hits.

A divorced man's brother dies in an industrial accident. Unions are a good idea.

A divorced man interacts with a gay man. Civil unions are a bad idea.

A divorced man wants to start dating again. His mother dies a week later.

A divorced man loves his hometown, but wants to move deeper into the Australian outback. If he moves he may never see his son again.

A divorced man wants to go surfing, like he used to, back when things were better, but his board comes off the roof of his car while he's on the M1. He goes anyway, and screams on the shore.

A divorced man starts a social AFL team with his friends. He kicks the winning goal two minutes after the game.

A divorced man never knew his daughter. When they meet, he gets too drunk and she vows to never see him again, even though he apologises a lot, over and over, both drunk and sober, inside the car and out. He promises her the world. He promises he will give her the world. She says: 'You've only got traditional Australian values, Dad.'

A divorced man receives a ticket for leaving debris on the M1. He'll deal with it after he's done drinking six tinnies on the back deck.

A divorced man's childhood hero dies. There is no state funeral, but he pours six tinnies out on the back deck for the great man anyway.

A divorced man never bloody knew about income tax. He drinks six tinnies on the back deck.

A divorced man goes camping in the Australian outback. He befriends two vaguely-European backpackers and learns something.

A divorced man goes to work and is confronted by a lack of job security typical for his demographic and line of work. He should have learned a trade. Out beyond the window, a tree is felled. He closes his eyes and sees his daughter in the car. Her makeup is running. He asks his boss about income tax.

A divorced man is kicked off his own social AFL team. 'Ha ha,' he says. 'Kicked off.'

A divorced man goes on an online dating site. A divorced man goes to the pub. A divorced man goes to the movies alone and looks for other people who are going to the movies alone.

A divorced man texts a divorced woman and asks when his son will be arriving today. Later, he drinks six tinnies alone on the back deck.

A divorced man goes fishing. He remembers when he was young always asking his own father when they could go home, and he wishes he had someone asking him the same thing.

A divorced man receives a follow-up letter regarding the debris he left on the M1. After six tinnies on the back deck he sends a reply.

A divorced man enters correspondence with an empathetic bureaucrat named Sally.

A divorced man walks down the road. He sees construction work; he sees shoes tied over the powerline. His town is not what it used to be.

A divorced man is sending continuous letters to an empathetic bureaucrat named Sally. The openings of her letters move quickly from 'To the owner of vehicle with registration number 211ASB' to 'Dear Fred' to 'My dearest darling Fred'. They correspond for a while. Sally replaces a bureaucratic number in one letter with her phone number, which begins with 04, and the divorced man calls her. They have phone sex, once, and he feels empty afterwards and hangs up. Sally keeps calling him and he just lies there. When he goes to call her back, his wireless landline has run out of battery.

A divorced man tries to sustain a long-distance relationship. He tries to install Skype, but finds that technology clashes with his traditional Australian values.

A divorced man tries to buy plane tickets online. His computer won't load the sites fast enough, so he goes to Flight Centre. The Flight Centre lady says: 'What are you going to be doing in Canberra?' and the divorced man says: 'I am going to visit my long-distance girlfriend.' The Flight Centre lady says: 'That's nice.' The divorced man says: 'Do you want to get a drink sometime?' The Flight Centre lady marks up his flights without telling him, and takes the bonus for herself.

A divorced man is with his son. He explains to his son that he might have a new Mum soon. His son says he already has a perfectly good mum, and that this situation interferes with his preconceptions of the ideal Australian family.

A divorced man explains to his son that two mums are better than one. He reminds himself that one mum would have been nice.

A divorced man's son isn't sure about a lot of things. A divorced man reminds him that civil unions are bad, and his son asks to go home.

A divorced man gets nervous before flying. He texts his friends apologising for not being able to make the game on Saturday. They remind him he is off the team. Tears gather on the rim of his seventh tinnie of the day.

A divorced man is met at Canberra Airport by a woman he has never met before. He goes to kiss her, but she only hugs him. He wonders how fast a return flight can happen. At the end of the story, she holds his hand.

A divorced man spends a week in Canberra. He wonders why anyone would prefer this place over the Australian outback. He asks his girlfriend and she says cities make her feel safe. He asks: 'Don't the trees make you feel safe? The horses and the bats? The spiders who are troubling but who are also your only friends?' and she says: 'No.'

A divorced man buys flowers for his girlfriend and sets them up in a vase on her table. He rearranges them as he thinks about his son and his daughter. He goes the toilet and he is still there, crying, when his girlfriend, the empathetic bureaucrat named Sally, comes home. She says: 'You leave tomorrow.'

A divorced man has sex with his girlfriend. This is the whole story.

A divorced man wakes up, walks around an apartment, looks for any trees at all out the window, and then dresses. He gets a lift to the airport. His girlfriend says: 'I don't think we should do this anymore.'

A divorced man gets nervous before flying. He texts his friends apologising for not being able to make the game on Friday. They remind him he is still off the team. Tears gather on the rim of his eighth tinnie of the day.

A divorced man returns home to the Australian outback after some time away. He feels disoriented and the story hints at depression without ever naming it. The bartender delivers a monologue about traditional Australian values.

A divorced man goes back to work after some time away. His boss breaks some news.

A divorced man feels his loyalty has been betrayed, and that he doesn't understand his own country anymore. He calls a lot of people's landlines. Many are disconnected. He doesn't understand why any of this has happened.

BRIANNA BULLEN
Apollo Bay Short Story Competition

A CONVERSATION BETWEEN EQUALS ABOUT *THE HUMAN CONDITION*

Two clones walk into a bar; this is not a joke but the beginning of my existential crisis.

Actually, perhaps I do joke—it was a café.

You, fiend, wear the same coat as me: identical brand labels, identical patterns. Grey trim on white, a reversal of the white snow trimming the grey footpath we trudge along. Realistically, you would not have known about our double-up. Irrationally, I feel comfortable in conformity as we walk from the opposite ends of the street—same cold-muted expression, subtly different feminine gaits—to meet in the centre, reverse mirrors crashing in a hug. Our breaths mingle in the cold air, heat buzzing from our chests out through layers of taut muscle and stiff fabric. We hold for a beat—I feel three heartbeats pulse evenly, a healthy product—until we are both uncomfortable by the uncommon materiality of the contact. We move from metaphase to anaphase, splitting apart from the centre, comfortably two individuals again and not a singular whole. You smile, a lazy upbeat movement lacking self-consciousness—the tight origami fold line of your mouth spreads out, revealing the paper-flesh has two sides, one red, one white. You wear CosmiTech's Oxygenated Red on those lips. It looks good on us. I reflect your smile with my own. 'Shall we?' Snow fades into our white-coated shoulders; you shiver, our bodies not habituated to such variation in temperature. Snowflakes blend in, looking like dandruff from a distance, but this close I can make out a difference. Your biology does not dissolve, fragmented though it may be. I look for individual differences before they melt—the snowflake myth a delectable favourite—but in the morning light I can barely see.

Propagated and percolated. Genetically modified and modifying. Morning coffee remains the twenty-second century's most archaic and widespread cultural practice. Every day, eight o'clock. It's been company mandate since 2097. All major businesses partake; a content workforce makes working content. The automated glass doors of the *Caffeine Stop* part for us, and I follow you, one step behind. We take a seat by the window, looking out at the sterile streets, neat footpaths parallel to neatly dividing traffic lines. Divide on divide on divide. The skyscrapers sprout, obscene phalluses, on the other side of the road, forming vertical lines ninety degree adjacent to the even horizon. The only variation between them is slight—some have a few more storeys than others. All have the same Plasma screen smooth windows; all face out to get the same views, only difference a slight alleviation in height and angle. Shared experience is something to be revelled in; yet, I wish there were trees to disrupt its perfection. These days I dream in lines.

The barista comes over, mechatronic, eyes brimming with stand-by blue static in his perfectly sculpted face, and you order our usual. We hear the click as our numbers are marked off. This close, I can see the blue dead tree veins at your temple. The porcelain sheen of the skin coating your high cheeks. The cherubic dimples, coded in creases, beside your mouth. Our generic heart-shape face from our model is shared by at least twenty-three others at our company. Genetic diversity stagnating, familiar 'pleasantness' is valorised. Sometimes, I doubt I have been meeting my same copy each morning for coffee. But as we wait, you check your Feed, hand turning the knob projecting its information into your ear. Your morning routine; getting informed confirms your identity. Possibly. I choose ignorance, looking up from the smooth black table to take in my usual view. The three baristas, interchangeable generic models, working in tandem in

monotone black behind the counter preparing coffees; the gathering line of bureaucracy that neatly breaks off at the door, each getting their numbers marked off the attendance sheet; the post-ironic 'No Smoking' sign, the only character in the room, neon-flashing on the wall, a relic from a time when self-destruction wasn't illegal; and us in the mirror, made quadruple. I watch the barista serving us come back with our flat whites, putting it down in front of the mirror-me. Time seems to move more slowly in that reflective world, everything uncannily flipped that little bit. It makes me take my time to re-find my physical self, the right hand to grasp the coffee with, as I stare at that not-Me. I lift it to my mouth. Perfect temperature, always. I lap at the edge, rim smooth against the ridges of my tongue. Lukewarm. Beige in flavour and colour. Technically perfect. I search for words that are my own, and not somebody else's, in my mental database. I don't know why, or what, I want to speak, but I do.

'I remember the day I came into the world. Consciousness erupted into artificial light. White bursting from the centre. Echoing out. Its streaks birthday streamers. I like the myth. Birthdays. Celebration. It must have happened. Once upon a time. Fairy tales: the history of their world. I cannot conceive. How could children rapture out from women? (You—attempt to—correct me in rupture.) Born in blood: a random patchwork of genes and parts in their red coats. Messy. Imprecise. Occasionally there would be a duplicate. Carbon copy clone through chance. Twins. Differences from a private space, the 'womb,' imprinting faults on the fingers. Glitches in unity known as the 'finger print.' I know I am rambling. Provoking.

A coffee cup clatters. You're looking at your fingers, aren't you? Smoothed out digits. No imperfections, no indentations, save the coffee stains which I mirror in my smile.

'Such barbarism', you tap one of those perfect fingers on the tabletop. 'It wasn't natural—live births. They never would have been able to comprehend. Sixty identical babies, engineered in a lab.' Your tone is the even of boredom, your face visual flat affect. I might be searching for depths where there is none, but there must be some interest if you are continuing to add to my strained, corrupted data deluge of a conversation.

'Do you remember our reception room? White walls with hyper-realistic paintings of nature, encased in glass. A Poplar behind a pane. Browning and balding leaves tumours proliferating then dropping away—'

'On a calm blue background. No, they weren't paintings. They were actual trees viewed through consecutive windows. Organic as you and me.'

Your static crackles threatening to produce a new image in your mind in this upheaval. My challenge on our shared memory system is met with resistance. Our possibly too-blue eyes remain locked. 'I believed they were paintings. Mistook them first for photographs, but then I noticed one was distorted, blue and green watercolour trickling down the image. Ruined illusion.'

'Wrong again. It was starting to rain outside, blue sky giving way to grey. Clear static streams. Liquid stalactites down the window. Room impregnated with staccato stammers, replacing the void silence with their semiotic cold communication.' I lean forward to look into your sleep-cushioned eyes, inhaling burnt coffee and cringing. Olfactory rejection.

'I recall the sun.'

Warmth. Alien echo. Perhaps the heating was on in our room, it seems familiar—remembered on my skin. But wrong. I look from you, smoothing your hair down like ink putty in your hands, to the window again. A factory's chimney rests against a smoke pillow and my eyes immediately dart to 'No Smoking.' 'I remember watching two raindrops race, transparent liquid cells moving slowly down on fragmented feet, water extending in two trudging points underneath the main ball. Both were making their way down slowly, neck-and-neck, until one joined a bigger drop, knocking it into an assembling network and disrupting it into a steady flow. The drops absorbed into each other and fell, lightening striking down the window pain as a clear vein.'

'How does one recall something so clearly so young? The images are contradictory. One must be wrong.' You laugh, a fractured jolt from unease.

I finish my coffee. 'Or they could both be right. Is it actually the same day being recalled? Perhaps we were kept for longer than one day, suspended.' I still live in vitro.

'Yes, I remember it just being the

one day clearly. Standard procedure. But now I'm doubting. They must have been windows, of a sort.' Your fingers tuck hair—black and severely bob cut, even more distinct lines—behind your seashell-swirl ear. Our nervous gesture.

'I do remember the sun though. It must have been a faint sun shower.' I concede, your struggles felt as my own.

'There must have been a rainbow mirage soon after, if they weren't paintings.'

'I have photographs from the day, haven't looked at them in years. The doctor took them for me. Scientist Magritte.' I play with my own hair; identically cut, it lacks your maintenance. Split ends. Growing offshoots. I should cut it.

'Was that his name? I thought it was different. Sometimes he sends me Christmas cards. Archaic practices long obsolete. The internet's victim. Overwritten code.'

'He wore a white coat and carried a brown teddy bear.'

'And wore a red scarf.'

You pause. 'I thought it was blue.'

'No, red.'

'It must have been red. Right, I remember now. His red coat.'

Codes disentangled, you nod a farewell and leave for work, worries of difference eased into pleasant nothing. It is too easy to get you to give into my version of reality; you acquiesce for your own desire for a life shared. Discontinuity promises defeat, but you think you have set us back into order. I sit for a moment, wavering between the dashed cigarette reflection in the window, and my empty mug. Yours remains untouched.

PENNY O'HARA
June Shenfield Poetry Award

THIRD DAUGHTER

my coal-lump, my combat vehicle
your bayonet gaze knows where it's going
your body better believe it

bomb-footed, poker-eyed
shot through with yang—christ
help the frame that tries to contain you

thunder-mouthed, tender brute
you'll make the round hole square
if it kills us

my steel-plated, ten-star general
my thorny grenade—whose fierce love
can only be met in kind

An ekphrastic poem after John Brack's Third daughter, *1954,*
National Gallery of Australia

THE POWER OF SNAILS

I turned vegetarian that summer we stayed with Antonio's uncle, Tío Juan, in his village, Tricio. The air was dry and thick and dust billowed when you kicked the ground. Children ran and shouted in Castellano along the cobbled streets, unaffected by the dry heat that slackened their parents.

Tío Juan liked to collect snails from the fields. From his basket, he'd pour them into a black crate lined with mesh, flicking the ones that clung to the sides so they dropped into the mess of brown.

The hundred-odd in there crawled, slid and furled into their shells, making scratchy sounds as they dragged themselves around the corners of the cramped space, trying to find an escape. When they knocked against each other, they clicked like marbles.

Their desperate movements became the chorus of my nights as I tossed in sweat-damp sheets that clung with the consistency of glue. Antonio, accustomed to the heat, lay sprawled in his underwear next to me, snoring lightly. I tried to close the door to the interior patio where the crate was set but the air was so suffocating, I leapt to open it not ten minutes later.

In the morning, I watched from a gap between the curtains as Tío Juan threw in a handful of breadcrumbs and shredded lettuce and spritzed the crate with water.

Caracoles para merendar mañana, he called, catching sight of me. Tomorrow, we feast on snails. He laughed, a hoarse, baritone chuckle that passed through his nicotine-yellow moustache and echoed around the patio. When he went back into the kitchen I slipped out, the chill of the terracotta tiles sending welcome shivers through my limbs. The sounds from the crate increased as I approached.

I lifted the lid, recoiling when my fingers brushed against the cold slime that coated the inside. Their shells created a mountain range of caramel and brown. Trails sparkled and crisscrossed around the cage. Some scrunched up fearfully within their shells while others stretched across the walls like discarded chewing gum. A few were copulating. Black droppings dotted the base where wilted lettuce and stale bread chunks lay.

'Careful,' Antonio said from behind me. I jumped back. The lid dropped with a clatter. He picked it up and secured it tightly.

'Don't creep up on me like that!'

'I only meant,' he said, touching my arm, 'that snails are strong. They can push the lid off if it's not shut properly. You know there's a snail race here, where kids harness sardine cans to their pet snails and see which one crawls the furthest in five minutes? They can get pretty far. My own pet snail came second one year.'

'Did you eat it afterwards?'

He ignored this. 'We'll need to leave the house when Tío Juan is cooking them. Their boiling mucous turns the kitchen into a stinking steam room. Maybe I can show you the monastery in Nájera or the Frank Gehry wine museum in Elciego.'

Shuddering, I pictured the snails scrabbling in a pot of simmering water, shrieking with pain in tiny, shrill voices.

—

During siesta time, I lay motionless in bed, sweat dripping from my arms and forehead. The snails were stupefied by the afternoon heat too, with hardly a sound coming from their prison. No breeze blew. The streets were empty of children's laughter and the usual kicks of footballs being passed around.

After the sun had set, I crept out to see them one last time. The evening was cooler and heavy inkblot clouds were spreading across the sky. The snails looked pitifully small in the dark. I plucked one from under the crate lid and placed it in my palm. Its foot was feathery against my skin, almost ticklish as it rippled across my hand. Bringing it closer, I stared into its tentacled eyes. They reached out to me in a silent plea. I saw its body, bathed in stew and chunks of tomato, saw myself prising it out of its shell with a toothpick and chewing down on its rubbery form. Smelled the chorizo, garlic and a briny, indefinable tang.

My stomach rolled. I wondered if I could ever eat any animal again, let alone this helpless, crawling mollusc with its long, sad eyes.

—

That night, it rained. The splatters of water brought a cool breeze and for the first time in weeks I slept without waking.

The roars of Tío Juan bellowed through the patio the next morning. Beside me, Antonio jumped out of bed with a startled shout. A snail clung to his forearm. There was a crunch. Our walls were dotted with spherical balls of swirled brown, each attached to a silvery trail. Outside, the crate lid was pushed to one side and I knew it would be empty. I closed my eyes and felt the coolness of dawn and the soft mist of evaporating rain on my skin.

It was not my day to try *caracoles*.

ALL THE WRONG THINGS

My father said our new neighbour looked like a bad apple and my mother let her eyebrows say what she wouldn't allow her mouth to utter.

It was Saturday, breakfast time. A van dropped off a young Aboriginal man with straight shoulders and bright chestnut eyes in front of the house on our right. He moved in with only a couple of duffle bags and a few boxes. I saw books and magazines in one, and a toaster and electric kettle in the other. An orange dog with white paws trotted after him.

'Didn't think I'd see his kind in our street.' A mix of anger and fear coloured my father's voice. 'Us Yugos and the Greeks, we're vanishing. Now with these two mongrels here,' he gestured with his thumb over his shoulder, 'the street is a bloody rainbow nation.'

That was when my mother's eyebrows started their dance. Her nostrils widened and half a snort escaped. My father craned his neck left and right, looking out the window.

'What's he looking our way for?' His eyes popped out like someone was after him.

My mother said, 'Esma, let's say g'day to our new neighbour before Alice comes.'

Alice, my school friend, helped me get an interview for a part-time job in Safeway on Main Road West where her brother-in-law was the assistant manager. I had to be at the store at midday.

'You're going to talk to that darkie?' my father spat out. 'Aren't you scared for our daughter's safety?'

'You're scared of all the wrong things,' my mother said as we stepped out.

Our new neighbour's name was Joe and he was from a community called Eden, somewhere up north in red dirt country.

'Where I'm from,' Joe said, 'there are only two colours; red under your feet and blue above your head. And there's black of course.' Joe ran his palm along his forearm and looked at our house.

He then stuck two fingers in his mouth and whistled, bringing his dog out from somewhere behind the house.

'This is Kanji. He almost never barks,' Joe said.

Kanji was tall and slender with a broad head that stood on his strong neck, which was nearly as thick as his hindquarters. He came to us ambling carefully and gently sniffed our outstretched hands. He lifted his head and his brown, ancient eyes observed us intently. He then turned swiftly on his big paws and walked away. His tail curved high over his back. He stopped under the apricot tree where he sniffed the ground and walked in tight circles readying himself to lie down. Before he assumed a resting position something alerted him. Kanji looked up lifting his muzzle in the air, his lean muscles stretching his shiny orange coat.

'He's never been in the city. Too much of everything at the same time,' Joe said.

'Put him on a leash or in the shed tonight. Saturday nights can get wild in our street,' my mother said.

Hook Street was long, flat, wide and straight, and because of this the hoons came in their souped up Falcons and Commodores, tyres burning the bitumen, beer cans flying through the open windows. The residents complained to the council. Not just about the noise and lack of sleep, but about their children being scared and their pets bolting in terror into the night. The police were called regularly. There was talk about putting speed bumps on the street, but nothing came of it. In the morning, the street would be covered with burnouts, vomit, urine, fast-food wrappers, and bottles of grog.

'I've seen the burnout marks,' Joe said and my mother and I nodded.

When we came back to the house my father rushed at us. 'That's a one hundred per cent pure dingo.' His voice was full of conviction as if he was brought up in the outback and not in the concrete jungle of communist flats in Yugoslavia.

'His name is Kanji,' I said.

'Kanji!' My father let out a scream, but the ring of the telephone cut him short.

It was my aunt Farah. We talked a little, and then she asked to speak with my father. She said, 'Girl, is your father home?' Aunt Farah said the word girl like that was my name.

My father was expecting the call. A couple of months ago Aunt Farah had lost her job and was having money troubles, had to sell her car, and couldn't make repayments on her home loan.

Brother and sister talked for a minute and at the end, through his clenched teeth, my father said, 'I'll let you know.'

When he hung up, he yelled, 'She's moving to Sydney, wants to drop off something for Esma before she leaves.'

'You know my answer,' my mother said from the kitchen.

At eleven Alice came to my house and she and my mother helped me with my outfit for the interview. My mother picked a light purple boat-neck top with a baby blue jacket and knee-length skirt. She arranged my hair in a bun and let me wear make-up. She said the outfit's colours went with my blue eyes, blonde hair and red lips. Alice held my hand and said I looked gorgeous. She ran her fingers along the collar of my top touching the exposed skin of my neck and collarbone.

My mother smiled. 'You both look gorgeous. A long-haired blonde and a pixie-cut brunette. A perfect combination.'

Alice warned me about her brother-in-law. 'He's a perv,' she said.

At the interview he only asked me if I had a problem handling pork products. I told him I had applied for a position in the grocery department, not the deli. He said that he'd transfer me as soon as he could. I remained quiet and stared back at him. I did my own version of the eyebrow dance. After a minute he sighed deeply, stood up and moved to the corner of his desk. He was half a metre away from me and his head hovered over mine.

He leaned in, put on a conspiratorial face and whispered, 'I'm short-staffed in the deli. Frankly I'm desperate. It's a fairly hard slog in there, cutting all those salamis and making sure the fish is tucked into ice. I'll give you two dollars extra per hour but not a word to anyone. Not even Alice. What do you think?' He extended his hand.

'I have no secrets from Alice,' I said, leaving his arm hanging in the air.

'I figured,' he said. 'I'll make sure she gets a pay rise too.'

I accepted his hand and we shook on it. When I was about to pull out of the handshake he put his other hand on top of my hand and clasped it. He stopped shaking the hand, and then stretched his thin lips, which revealed his gapped teeth. I freed my hand when his touch became uncomfortable and thanked him for giving me the job. He said no problems, and stuck his hands into his pants, resting his thumbs on his belt.

Alice waited for me outside the store. I told her everything.

'That arsehole. You want me to sort him out?' Alice asked with a frown on her face. I shook my head.

Alice had a shift starting at one o'clock so we agreed to meet up the next day to celebrate. She kissed me on the cheek before I left.

Sunday afternoon I was getting ready to meet Alice when I heard my father's voice coming from outside. I peeked through the window and saw him talking to Joe.

'His mutt took off last night,' my father said when he walked back into the house. 'Wants us to keep an eye out.'

Outside I told Joe I could help him put up missing dog posters when I returned.

'I don't have any photos of him.' Joe looked at the sky and then at me. 'He'll find his way back,' he said.

When Alice and I returned to my house it was almost fully dark. My father came into my room. I told him about my new job and Alice's pay rise. His eyes were fixed on Alice's. She endured my father's stare before peeping beyond his burning gaze. Then her body trembled and she stood up.

'It's getting dark. Better be on my way,' she said.

'Your friend looks like a boy,' my father said during dinner and then added that Alice looked like she was trouble. He referred to Alice in the same cold, angry voice he used when referring to my Aunt Farah. There was wild fear in his eyes just like yesterday when he saw Joe.

While my mother and I ate he kept tapping his tablespoon on the side of the soup bowl. A few times he lifted the spoon and opened his mouth, but he stopped short of swallowing.

'I don't want Farah and her kind disturbing this household,' he said through his teeth, his fists clenched and resting on the table on either side of his bowl.

My mother put her index finger on her lips and said, 'Eat. The soup is getting cold.'

He brought the spoon to his mouth only to drop it in the bowl. The hiss came out of his serpent mouth, 'She's unwed.'

On the few occasions we visited my aunt we saw signs of the other woman living in the house. During those visits Aunt Farah would ask my parents about swimming classes, learning to ride a bike or taking karate lessons instead of my dance classes. My parents would insist that she stop calling me girl and call me Esma. She would just wave them off and say, 'It doesn't suit her. She's no Esma.' She would deflect my parents' protestations by taking me out on pretence of going for an ice cream but instead she let me drive her car.

While I struggled with the clutch and the accelerator causing the car to bunny hop she'd put her hand on my hand manoeuvring the gearstick, giving me instructions.

'First, the important things needed for survival. Swimming, driving, self-defence, knowing how to spot a prick,' she told me once. 'Forget dancing. Dancing won't help you if someone jumps you in the middle of the night.'

'Not planning on walking by myself in the middle of the night.'

Aunt Farah put her hands on my cheeks. Her lips formed into a line. 'Girl, they don't care about the time of the day. It's your job to be ready.'

When we returned from the drive she always made me stand next to the doorframe in the kitchen where she marked my height. It was part of this doorframe she wanted to give me before leaving for Sydney.

As we ate in silence I thought about Alice. Yesterday, after my job interview, we bought a large strawberry milkshake at the 7-Eleven on Station Road. We walked over to Jamieson Street Park and sat inside the plastic castle, a part of the children's play equipment.

We drank the milkshake from the same straw and talked about things we would buy and concerts we wanted to go to. Alice took my hand and I felt my heart go calm and my breathing slow down. She leaned over and very tenderly wiped a line of foam from my top lip. I took both her hands, brought them to my lips and kissed them. Alice pulled me into her embrace, our faces nearly touching. I stroked her hair, her cheeks, and our lips joined in our first kiss.

Afterwards we put our heads through the small windows of the castle. Tiny, cold droplets of rain pricked our warm faces. We watched the tall, skeletal gum trees dotting the edge of the footpath in pairs, their branches touching. Behind one of the trees an orange dog with white paws appeared.

I asked Alice to whistle.

KATELIN FARNSWORTH
Verandah Genre Award 2017

LOLLIES

Mrs Gauson had black frizzy hair that draped around her shoulders and made me think of wriggly worms. She said she was excited to have me in her class. I was excited too and I arranged my pencil case neatly and looked around the room. There were coloured posters on the walls and tubs of cardboard and glue on the the tables. Mrs Gauson's face was shiny and she wore pink lipstick. She smiled a lot and every time she smiled the lipstick on her mouth seemed to crack a little. I wondered why she wore it at all. 'Just like your brother,' she told me. 'You'll be top of the class, I know it!'

I shrugged and sucked on my pen lid. My brother was an *intellectual*. He won awards and went to special classes where men with balding heads clapped him on the back. My brother won scholarships to expensive private schools. He read science books for fun and he knew how to calculate big numbers. I was still learning my times table and could barely remember how to spell my name.

The first time I failed a spelling test Mrs Gauson pulled me aside.

'Are you ill?' She pushed her tiny glasses up her nose. 'Is there something wrong? You can talk to me about anything.'

But I couldn't open my mouth. There were words in there, stuffed at the back of my throat, but none of them would come out. 'I dunno. I'm fine. Sorry. I'll do better next time.'

Mrs Gauson narrowed her eyes but then nodded, as if relieved by my answer. If there was something wrong with me she didn't want to know about it.

Next time it was a maths test. The numbers spread out across the page and stared up at me like tiny ants. I wished they were ants. That they would scuttle away. I traced my fingers around the black figures and tried to imagine what they could possibly mean.

4 x 6

6 x 4

3 x 5

Mrs Gauson hovered over me. 'What's going on?' she barked.

I touched the side of my face. 'I'm tired.'

'What? Your brother never got tired.'

I held the sheet of paper up.

'I don't know how to do these,' I told her. 'They make my head hurt.'

'Your head hurts?'

I nodded and she looked at me as though I wasn't making sense. For a second I wondered if I was. And then I wondered who decided what made sense or not. Because, somebody, somewhere, had decided that these maths sums made sense but I didn't see what right they had to decide that.

'Well maybe you should go to sickbay,' Mrs Gauson said doubtfully, still looking at me in astonishment.

'It's not that kind of hurting,' I told her, sweeping the piece of paper off the desk. 'I just don't understand these questions.'

'They're simple questions. We've been over all of this.'

'But I don't understand any of it. It doesn't make sense to me.'

'How can it not make sense?' Mrs Gauson looked confused, her hand scratching at her face, and I thought about answering, of trying to put into words what I saw when these numbers were placed in front of me. But I knew that, just the way a part of me couldn't make sense of the times table, Mrs Gauson couldn't make sense of me.

I sat up at the wooden desk and listened as Mrs Gauson shouted out numbers. She wrote complicated patterns on the black board and shook her head when I slumped. Her face crumpled when I brought her the wrong answers.

'I think you might need some extra help,' she told me one afternoon. The sun was shining in through the blinds and my face felt hot. I touched my cheeks with my hands and tried to avoid Mrs Gauson's eyes.

'No,' I whispered. Shaking my head from side to side slowly. Mrs Gauson held up my work book. I stared at the red marks across it.

'You've got all these questions wrong, Katie.'

I didn't like the way she said my name. I felt tiny and I dropped my hands into my pockets and looked towards the window. There were birds swinging round in the sky. I looked at their black shapes and wondered if baby birds had maths lessons somewhere too. Mrs Gauson's voice cut through my thoughts.

'I can tutor you after school if you like. I'll talk to your parents. I think it will be good for you.'

I shook my head again and thought about my brother. At home he was reading *The Lord of the Rings*. After dinner each night he would spread the book out across his lap and giggle to himself. I wondered if I'd ever be like him. Able to get lost inside books, able to sit there by myself and laugh at imaginary creatures. I longed for it. But the alphabet was hard to remember and long words were difficult to understand and Mrs Gauson kept telling me I wasn't up to scratch and I was beginning to believe her.

'I don't want to be tutored.' The words slid out of my mouth before I had thought them through.

'What? Why not?'

'I dunno,' I mumbled. I felt like I was on fire. I wondered if my whole body was made of flames. What would happen if my insides opened up? Would the whole room suddenly be engulfed with flames? Mrs Gauson would die. All the other children would die. Their faces would come apart. Their eyes would pop out of their sockets and roll around on the floor. Their mouths would peel off their faces and flap. I imagined the smell of hair burning. I touched my own hair. Twisted it slowly around my finger.

'Katie?'

Mrs Gauson was looking at me. She put down my workbook and sighed. 'It's going to be okay,' she said. 'We'll get you help.' Her voice was gentle and it sailed out into the air softly.

I tried to think of something to say. I wanted to tell her that I wasn't stupid. But suddenly I didn't know if I was. What if I was stupid? What if I had always been stupid? What if I was destined to be stupid for the rest of my life? Because hadn't I struggled learning how to tie my laces? Didn't I find it utterly impossible to tell the time on an analogue clock? And maps confused me. Sometimes I forgot my left from right. Maybe my head was full of all the wrong parts. Maybe my head was broken and there was nothing any one could do for me. I imagined doctors in white coats hanging over me. Opening my head and staring down into it. I imagined doctors leaning forward and shrugging.

'There's nothing we can do,' I heard them saying. 'Her head doesn't work. It's full of all the wrong parts. It's inoperative. Sorry.'

But even though they said sorry they didn't care. Their jaws shook as they chewed gum. They laughed and pushed their eyes together. They sealed my head up and sent me out on my way.

Mrs Gauson brought lollies to the tutoring sessions. Jelly babies and rainbow coloured jelly snakes. She set them down in a plastic container on the side of the desk. Every time I got a question right I got to eat one.

'It's an incentive,' she said. When I didn't respond she sighed. 'Do you know what an incentive is?'

'I dunno.' I kicked my legs up and down under the table.

At home my parents were getting my brother ready for a special test. If he did well in this test they were going to get a lot of money. My mum said the money would really help. She said they'd be able to pay for more tutoring lessons for me.

Mrs Gauson picked up a pen and started scribbling. I watched the way the pen moved, scratching up and down, and I closed my eyes. In the darkness I saw shapes, and the shapes danced. I liked the way the shapes moved. They were colourful too. Blobs of purple and blue. Somewhere, in the faint distance, I could hear Mrs Gauson chattering but I was more interested in the shapes. They were my friends.

'And then the five goes here and we multiply it by two, you see?'

I opened my eyes. The plastic container of lollies was full to the brim. I nodded.

'I see,' I told her.

'Do you? Say it back to me.'

I hesitated. 'I see shapes inside my head,' I said instead.

'What?'

'Shapes,' I repeated. 'Blue and purple. I like purple.'

'What are you talking about?'

'I don't want to do maths. I want to draw shapes.'

Mrs Gauson leaned in and I could see all the wrinkles on her face. She crinkled her forehead.

'Shapes? What sort of shapes?' she asked.

'Any kind! All shapes.'

'I think we should concentrate on this,' she said, tapping at the work book with a long finger. Her nails were painted red. I wondered if I should paint mine red.

'When can I go home?'

'Not yet. We need to get this into your head.'

'Okay.'

But I knew we would never get any of it into my head. Whatever went into my head just fell right out again. It slipped out of my ears and onto the ground.

'You know,' Mrs Gauson said one afternoon a few weeks later. The classroom was empty except for us. Outside the winter sun had already set. 'You're not really grasping any of this, are you?'

I looked up at her and felt tears flood my eyes.

'Not really.' I spoke into my hand. 'But I'm trying.'

'Oh, Katie.' She smiled. But it was a strange kind of smile; a smile that's not really a smile at all. 'I know you are.'

'Yeah.'

And then we were silent and I stared at the tub of lollies and wondered if I'd ever get to eat one.

'The other kids think I'm stupid,' I said after a while. 'Do you think I'm stupid? My brother says I'm stupid.'

'You're not stupid.'

'Are you sure?'

'You're not stupid,' she repeated.

And her words swung out of her mouth and fell into the air and I watched them and I shivered and I bent my arm out and tried to catch the word 'stupid'. I grabbed hold of it and cradled it between my arms, pretending it was a baby.

'You just struggle with numbers. It's okay. It's not the end of the world,' she said.

'Really?'

'Really.'

Mrs Gauson's eyes were wet. She reached across the desk for the tub of lollies.

'Here,' she said. 'Have a lolly.'

'But I didn't get any of the questions right.'

'It doesn't matter. Take a lolly.'

Something inside my chest moved. I pulled out an orange and red snake and stared at it. I wrapped it around my little finger before popping it into my mouth. It tasted good. Sweet and sour; soft between my teeth. Mrs Gauson reached one for too. When I had finished mine, she handed me another.

'You're not stupid,' she said again.

I ate my lolly in silence and nodded.

KAREN ANDREWS
2017 Alan Marshall Short Story Award (local division)

MIRIAM AND MILDRED

Miriam hitched her skirt and kneeled beside the cow. The animal made a mournful noise and in reply, from the nearby holding yard, came the bleat of her calf. Miriam could picture its pretty brown and white face against the palings, tendrils of spit dripping from its mouth. Rather than milk, she had the urge to place her hand over her ears and block all entreaties. Not that it mattered—those sounds were already committed to her soul. Miriam shifted her weight, placed her hands on the rubbery udders and got her elbow ready just in case the cow had a tantrum. Empathy was one thing, a broken foot another. They would just have to pass this time together in their mutual poor mood. Miriam's insides felt like they were curdling. This last cow— Mildred, she'd secretly named her—and she would be done.

There came the pearled stream, a metallic ping. Again and again she squeezed, feeling sicker each time.

'You still here?'

Her father's voice, a cacophony of accusation under the tin roof.

'I started late.'

'May I ask why?'

One of Mildred's ears flicked at his mock politeness.

'I don't feel well.'

Miriam heard him mutter to himself as he surveyed the dairy, stopping to inspect if each empty stall had been left to his satisfaction. As he approached, her uterus seized again. Oh, no. Miriam clenched every muscle she could between her legs. If anything, it made the pain worse. And it didn't make a difference. The bleeding began, taking to liberty with gusto. She looked down. Blouse, thin skirts. It was warm.

'Good yield today?' she asked loudly, looking for a distraction. God, it hurt. May the Lord forgive her for taking his name in vain, but it did. Was this how it struck all women? She had to stay seated until he left, and then get back to the house unnoticed to get her rags and change. But first problem first: act normal.

'Nearly done?' he asked, learning against the railing. Mildred turned at the sound of her father's voice, recognising her master. Yes, Joseph Fisher was the question-asker—not her, her brothers, not even her mother.

A band of muscles went into spasm across her stomach. 'Yes,' she said, struggling to keep an even tone.

'Samuel is expected for dinner.'

Miriam bit the inside of her cheek. 'I know.'

'I expect you to be more civil to him on this visit.'

Miriam suspected she had been as civil as any fifteen-year-old girl could be to a seventeen-year-old boy with a doughy, pale face, who made long eye-contact over the dinner table and had the disturbing talent of arranging to be momentarily alone in the same room. Her brothers couldn't even stand Samuel—they teased her when they were in the field, ghosting her from behind, standing so close she could feel their breath upon her neck. Turning to strike, they'd dance backwards and laugh, saying they were merely emulating her betrothed. It was a lie, of course. Their mimicry was born from the same mistrust of Samuel's unsettling energy.

'We are *not* betrothed,' she'd snap.

No, but she wasn't stupid. Samuel's family was influential in the community; not that they weren't, but Joseph had always felt that his had been overlooked. His belligerence, his scheming, was a source of suspicion. He was a man of the new century, he claimed, surrounded by people of the old. That required heeding to custom.

Like matchmaking.

'I'll do my best,' she said to her father, continuing to milk, hoping that her attentiveness to her job would be enough to assuage her father's problem with its lateness of completion.

She'd had a lot of experience in masking one reality with the semblance of another. Like hiding her monthly bleed for almost two years from everyone except her older cousin Rebecca, a stalwart ally who Miriam loved more than anyone else in the world. Rebecca had been subtly shunned by the town since she left to marry a man from the city more than five years ago. On a rare return in those early days, she handed over a package to Miriam containing everything she'd need to keep her womanhood a secret. Miriam's mother had done the same with dignified solemnity, but those rags remained unstained in her drawers, but not untouched. Her mother checked, she was certain.

Miriam just wanted time, that's all. Was that so much to ask? If her father knew she was bleeding now, he would be satisfied she was in good health. Another stage completed towards destiny. She rested her forehead against Mildred's belly and took a deep breath of animal mustiness. Theirs was a similar relationship and duty: of procreation and secretion.

Mildred's tail twitched in irritation—a fly, perhaps. Miriam sat back just in time to save the bucket being turned over as the cow stepped forward in the stall to adjust her position.

'Drat!' She raised her hand to swat Mildred as an exasperated anger suddenly filled her head, stopping at the last second to instead curl it into a fit and bring it back to her side. The keening of the calf outside began again.

'That's enough,' said her father. 'Let her out. Go see if your mother needs any help.'

Miriam's toes curled with indecision. What to do? She looked to the cow and an idea struck.

'Can you please go up and release the door to the yard? I'll walk her out.'

A strange request, but it was the best she could do. Her success laid in the balance.

'Temperamental beast,' said Joseph, tickling Mildred's ears as he walked past.

'She has her days.'

'I was talking about you.' Joseph pushed the bolt. It was rusted, making it sticky and he turned his back to concentrate on forcing it open.

Miriam seized her chance. She stood up and glanced at the stool, rubbing the blood smear off the surface with the hem of her skirt. She ducked behind the rump of the cow. Out of sight, she twisted her skirt around to inspect the spreading red starburst, not as large as she'd expected. She picked up the bucket and held it low over her stomach. It worked, covering the stain. But she would still need to be careful.

Joseph freed the latch and the door fell open. Mildred trudged forward, her emptied udders swayed back-and-forth out into the sunshine. Miriam gripped her bucket and followed the cow into the yard.

'Where are you going now?'

'I just want to check something. I won't be long.'

She heard her father grunt as she pushed the door back to be re-latched.

She breathed a sigh of relief as the bolt was secured, marvelling at her good fortune. Mildred trotted across the yard to her calf. Miriam turned away before seeing what she knew would come next: nose pressed to nose the animals would stand together, communicating hunger and desire.

Miriam rolled back her shoulders. One day she might feel the same way.

A day long off in the future, she hoped.

KELLY SIMPSON
*Stonnington Untitled Literary Festival Short Story Competition,
open age category*

VIEWPOINT

The water sluices around my body, the push of the waves impossible to resist. Each surge brings me closer to shore, and eventually I just surrender.

Push, pause, push, pause, and then one last thrust.

Ahh.

The warmth of the sand and sun is like a tonic. The grains of sand feel coarse on my skin, but the relief at not having to move reminds me of how close I have come once more to exhausting myself in the watery depths.

I decide to stay where the tide has deposited me, recharge my batteries, and when it comes for me again, I will be ready.

The lady slowly breast-strokes parallel to the shore, head bobbing above the waves. Her swim cap, and the matching goggles perched high on her head seem poised for action, but they remain completely dry.

As she scans back and forth, she can't help but notice a large cluster of people on the sand.

'What are they doing?' she asks herself, and the world, out loud.

She is compelled to investigate.

'What on earth?' she splutters loudly as she wades to shore. She looks around quickly. How can she have missed this? Something is going on, right in the middle of the beach, and she doesn't know what, and it almost kills her.

She accelerates.

Reaching the throng, she pushes and shoves her way through until she reaches yellow tape. She glances down, and for a moment, considers barging straight through. But her peripheral vision catches a grey shape in the centre of the tape.

'It's a seal!' she exclaims loudly, looking around to make sure everyone near her, and those not so near, know that she knows. Perhaps too she is telling people who may not know. She smiles with self-importance.

Of course, all these people, especially those she just pushed through, already know exactly what it is, and have been observing it with varying degrees of interest.

'Well, what we need is a trolley,' she proclaims loudly.

'A small platform with wheels,' she explains further, using her hands to demonstrate the shape in the air.

'Then we just wheel it to the ocean and it's all done.'

She claps her hands loudly, forcing people to turn and look at her.

'Who has a trolley?'

She pauses for a brief moment. No-one answers.

'Or a stretcher. We could fashion a stretcher from a towel and people could carry the seal to the water.'

She positively quivers with her excitement at solving the puzzle.

The girl trails after her parents, feet sinking into the warm grains of sand toes first, evaporating sea water leaving its tight salty residue on her skin.

There's talk of a seal on the beach, and she's curious. But she's also trepidatious.

Last time, the seal on the beach was sick, really sick. And it was a baby seal.

Kids ran past and poked it, and her Mum became indignant at their lack of respect.

Animals are her favourite. Any animal. Maybe not cows which are too big and too static, until they're not, and they become lumbering mountains of unpredictable flesh seemingly heading straight towards you.

But, oh, how she would love to swim with a seal. To know it was a seal, to be able to dive under the water, and see it glide. Imagining herself and her body scything through the water with the same grace and elegance.

The girl follows her parents, weaving politely between people until they too can see the slick grey shape lying on the shore.

Oh.

She turns and buries her face in her mother.

She feels her Mum's hands on the back of her head.

'It's okay darling, it's not sick, it's just tired.'

Really? She turns her head and risks a glance.

Maybe it is. It looks plump and shiny, not like the other time.

There's chatter around them, and she tunes into the voice of a woman wearing a hi-vis vest.

'… Antarctic crab-eating seal. About eighteen months old and kicked out of home, and just hasn't found his way yet. He tries to find food, and then gets too tired and comes ashore in the tide. At Torquay last week, and here at

Point Roadknight today.'

'Wow, did you hear that?' her Mum asks, knowing.

Her daughter looks up, her face aglow.

'Yes.'

The two young men run into the surf. One dives, and the other somersaults exuberantly into a wave.

'Did you post?' calls apricot boardshorts.

'Yeah,' comes the quick reply. 'Animals, man. Always crazy.'

They are waist deep, waves breaking around their tanned bodies, but their eyes are focused on the shore and the prize. The tide has almost reached its highest point, licking at the supine seal.

'Sixty-two likes already.'

'Shit, alright. I'll make sure I get it.'

He checks his GoPro.

They have been waiting hours for the tide to turn, when it hopefully takes the seal back out to sea. A chance to swim with it, try and beat it, maybe even stroke it. But most of all, capture the moment. Sixty-two likes already for a photo of a seal between the flags. Imagine how many for a photo of them in the water with the seal.

They move a little deeper, trying to navigate a path that is not obviously in breach of the cordoned area. They are ready.

The seal manoeuvres as each surge of water approaches, conserving his energy and using the water's momentum to reposition. He waits, feeling the welcome solidity of the beach beneath him, but longing now for the cool slickness and silence of underwater.

Yes, this should do it.

Freedom again.

FLYING TO IPSWICH
IN THE COMPANY   OF SAINT JACKIE HOWE

I promised you an adequate poem
Ipswich. But the one I unwrapped
in my cattle class seat was sub-grade:
too many dags & grass seed doubts.

I'm no gun shearer. My only chance
of clearing the terminal with a tally
within a bull's roar of decent is to stay
bent over this pad, working my blades,
dabbing tar on misplaced cuts, praying
Jackie Howe, unbeaten hand shearing
champion of the world, patron saint
of shearers, pressers & roustabouts
(soft pawed classers can look after
themselves) will lend a hand to fill
my pressurised shed with the music
of tumbling golden fleece.

I was raised on a soldier settler block:
stony paddocks, artesian bore, furnace
summers your Ipswich potters could
use for outdoor kilns. Enough covers
of occasional Mandrake green to keep
our flock of Corriedales fed until
world prices & interest rates ganged
up with shearers' wages to throat us
like a wild dog pack. On sale day Dad
took down his father's hand shears

& leaned low over our pet ewe
to give & receive the final blows.

———————

This new poem lambed an hour ago
when a flock of fresh-loomed
clouds mobbed around our wing,
floating, a spun white still life, as if...

a giant presser in the grip of a sky-shed
sulk over a breach of award conditions
had flung his fleece far & wide
& thumped away to complain
to his union rep. Who should I thank
for this vision & the eleventh hour
clip lifted from its back? I'd like
to think it was a bequest from
Saint Jackie Howe that's been biding
its time, waiting for a double shot
of deadline juice & some quiet
in my cattle class head to catch again

the music of hooves & dogs
&
get em in!   *get em in!*

clattering down a ramp.

Jackie Howe (1861–1920) set shearing records with blades (hand shears) that stood for over 50 years until the introduction of machine shears. His weekly tally of 1437 sheep in 44 hours 30 minutes remains unbeaten. He was a strong unionist and the first worker to wear the navy blue singlet which bears his name to this day. Pressers pack wool into bales. Classers classify categories of wool. A blow is a single sweeping cut through a sheep's fleece.

A SHOEBOX NOT FILLED WITH SHOES

The mother was no good with shovels, she'd said. He hadn't asked if they even *owned* one because it didn't seem likely and he didn't want to be a dick. It was something he was trying lately, a new leaf. He arrived at their place a few hours after school, and wondered if he should've put dinner on so something would have been ready by the time he got back. But he didn't know how long he'd be and didn't want to burn the house down yet. The shovel leant like an uncomfortable hand on his shoulder. He hadn't asked his mum if he could borrow it because he knew she would say no. But it wasn't hers anyway. He shuffled from foot to foot in gumboots two sizes too small. The door to his neighbour's place finally opened.

'Ah you're such a great lad.' The mother said upon seeing him with the shovel. He didn't know the woman by name, only that as a single lady, she was part of the same mothers' club that hung out at the arts centre café every Wednesday. Drinking one coffee every two hours and complaining about the skateboarders on the pavement outside.

'Oi you lot,' she now called into the depths of her house, 'scarper up. And bring Sooty!' Sooty, he assumed, was the dog, and for a brief moment he imagined a small child was just going to run up and chuck it in his arms, then step back, smiling. He gripped the shovel and wondered if he'd leave.

They appeared at the doorway, and he counted them without wanting to look like he was counting them. She had four children, potentially five but he couldn't see what was on the couch. They crowded around him, asking to hold the shovel (which he gave to them) and asking for money (which he ignored). The mother let them flow around her with the resignation of someone standing at low tide. He guessed they were aged between three and twelve and wondered if they were all from the same father, and then reminded himself that he wasn't being a dick. One of the younger ones came up to him holding a shoebox that he knew was not filled with shoes.

'Thanks again for this hun,' the mother said.

'No worries,' but he was trying to think when he first heard the news about their dog, and how long it had been sitting in the box for. He took it with one hand and held it like a child trying not to find out what their Christmas present was. A girl who looked older than the rest, maybe fourteen, was standing in a doorway that lead off to dark rooms. He nodded to her and she smiled, looked down and then glowered. He mentally shrugged and thought about the weight of the box in his hand. He'd heard that the dead things could freaking liquefy.

'You wanna come back here for a drink or something? After?' the mother asked him.

'Nah, thanks,' he said, gently trying to grab the shovel from the hands of a small child. 'I gotta get dinner. Cheers but.' The mother looked at the small game of tug of war happening at her feet.

'Oi, Tommy, get off that. The rest of you lot, get back inside.' She wore the same type of all-purpose nightgown that his mother did, the one that if you didn't look too closely you could maybe mistake for a dress. It clung to her the same way her husband didn't. He suddenly felt sad, or carsick.

'Anyway …' he said, shovel in one hand, boxed dog in the other. Nodding at the mother and the girl in the doorway. He backed out, screen door slamming behind him.

'Wait,' he heard a voice and thought it was meant for him, 'someone should go with him.'

'Why?' the mother was looking at the girl, 'it's not like he's going to *steal* it or something.'

'Nah. To pay respects, you know? Or

whatever.' And she folded her arms.

'Do what you like. But if you're not home for dinner that's your loss. You don't mind do ya?' the mother called to him, opening the screen again, 'she's not gonna get in the way?'

'Sure, nah it's fine,' and he hefted the dogbox under his arm in case she wanted to shake hands, but she just walked past the door as her mother held it open. He followed her into the cloying evening, wondering how deep he'd have to dig.

They walked without saying anything, and this was fine with him. He was busy trying to decide if he could get her to carry one of the things. The shovel was getting heavy, but it was pretty dirty and he couldn't change hands without putting the dog down. But he didn't want to pass the box to her either, it felt like he'd taken responsibility for it and that it was now his. It may also gross her out. They walked in the direction of the park, which he thought she might assume was where they were going to bury it. He'd decided earlier that he'd take it to the reserve though and do it proper. She didn't say anything as they passed the park though, and he wondered what she was thinking.

'What's your name?' he asked, to try and break the silence.

'Sherline,' she said, 'but you better not call me that.'

'Right,' he said, when she provided no alternative. 'I'm Jason, Jase, whatever.'

'Cool.' She said. The reserve was a couple of minutes away. He could've just buried it in the park, and that was probably what her family was expecting, but he didn't think that was right. His worst fear was having small kids just coming across it. Imagining them digging in the dirt and suddenly a dog corpse was there at their feet in whatever stage of decay. No, he'd much prefer the reserve. Dig deeper, less children.

'How old are ya?' she asked him after a while.

'Does it matter?'

'Nah, whatever.' And she was silent for a moment. 'I'm seventeen.' Which put her at about fifteen–sixteen depending on what bra she wore.

'Cool.' He said. She was three years too young for him, if he'd been looking. Which he reminded himself he wasn't. Part of this 'new leaf' bullshit was that he'd promised to stop screwing around. 'What kind of dog was it?' He didn't want to personalise the thing in the shoebox, but he struggled with silence, especially from a girl who he didn't know what she wanted.

'Him? Oh, he was a Boxer cross.' She looked at him funny, her face kinda crooked.

'Uh-huh,' Jase said, not knowing shit about dogs.

'Nah I'm just fucking with ya, it was a joke,' and she laughed, whether at him or at her joke he wasn't sure. 'Sif I know what he was.' And Jason laughed too, first because he didn't get it, then because he did, and then at the fact that she would make a joke like that about her dead pet, and then just at the image of the two of them just walking down the street, death in their arms, laughing.

They reached the reserve and Jase leant the shovel down and hopped the gate. The shoebox almost slipped out of his hand and he looked around to see if Sherline, or whatever, had noticed. But she'd gone around, walking through the proper way. His sister had always done that too. The gate clanged closed and he wondered why he was trying to impress her, or if he was. He hefted the shovel over and together they walked down the path. It wouldn't be dark for the next few hours, but already the scrubby bush looked uninviting. He only knew the place from when his old man would take him there on alternate weekends. It was close to where he'd use to live, and Jase assumed he had some kinda nostalgia or something about it. Jase had hated it. Or not really hated it, but just hated how he'd always spent the last few hours of his weekends here, watching his father walk down the path. It had been boring back then and it was boring now, even with the dead dog and the girl. The evening shadows gave it a hint of something though, and his shoulders ached from the shovel. Again, he wondered what she was thinking.

'Been here much?' he asked. She was a few steps behind him, and he slowed down to let her catch up and hoped it wasn't in an obvious way.

'Nah, not that much. You did alright but.' Jase frowned. 'In picking here I mean.'

'Yeah? How'd you figure that?' he tried to stay at the same pace as her.

'We took Sooty here a couple of times. He really loved it.'

'Sooty?'

'The dog ya dimwit.'

'Yeah nah I know, shit. I meant, why'd you call him that anyway?'

'I dunno, it was the kid's dog, they chose whatever.'

'Cool,' he said, trying to work out where he would bury Sooty. He picked an arbourtrary tree a little while down the path and told himself he'd have chosen a spot by then. He didn't think he could count on her to help.

'You get along with them then? The other kids?'

She didn't seem to like being called a kid, but said: 'Yeah, I guess. Not really.' And then was silent until he started walking off to the side of the path and started digging.

'What do ya want me to do?' she said as he drove the shovel again in the ground. Sooty was sitting in his box and from the trees came the noises of birds trying to get laid before nightfall.

'Nothing, it's all good. Does this look like an alright place?'

'Yeah sure,' she shrugged and he rubbed his shoulders for a bit and then started digging. At first the dirt was easy, light, mostly leaf litter and sticks. Part of him was keeping an eye out for any evening dog-walkers or something, in case he and Sherline looked suspicious. There was the ever-present paranoia of cops, walking past and seeing him digging a grave. *What the hell would they think?* he wondered. He tossed the dirt to the side and tried not to get it on the dogbox, but then he realised that it probably wouldn't matter in a few minutes. He smiled and shook his head. She'd found a log nearby and was sitting on that resolutely not watching him. The dirt got harder quickly, and started becoming clay. His hands were raw and he wondered why he hadn't just said stuff-it and done this at the park. If they'd had a backyard it would have been even easier. Jase wondered briefly if she'd brought any water which would've helped break up the clay too. As he dug he tried to think of something nice to say about the dog, but before today he hadn't even met the rest of the family, let alone their pet. He doubted she was expecting a proper funeral anyway.

'Do you smoke?' she asked after a while.

'Nah,' he said, concentrating on caving in the sides now so the hole became wider.

'I do,' he heard the flicking of a lighter and didn't bother looking up.

'Does ya mum know?' But she ignored him, obviously not wanting to lose the moment of the first drag.

'I took 'em from me dad, when he was around, but now it's harder to get. You know?' she said after a while.

Jason nodded but realised he could have been mistaken for just trying to get flies off his face so he said 'Yeah', and kept digging. She hadn't offered to help and he was glad. She hadn't offered him a cigarette either, but could probably sense his distaste. Normally he'd have taken his shirt off by now, but didn't feel comfortable with her around, so it was getting sweaty and dirt stuck to it like it was trying to get him back for something. She smoked in silence and the night started falling like an old old man who'd had too much to drink.

The hole was slowly getting bigger and he was reminded about when he'd seen his dad digging, all of about three times. This was back at the old place, and when he'd had time and it had been light enough outside, his father had gone outside and planted stuff, or just turned the soil around til it got dark. He never invited Jase to come, and it was only when he went outside to see where he'd gone that he saw what his father was doing. Digging, just digging. Something deeply aimless or ritualistic. Jase had first thought that he was trying to hide things and thought about going back later and seeing if he could find anything worth blackmailing, but in the end couldn't be bothered. It was his mother doing the cheating anyway. His father was just turning to soil, as if preparing graves for the children he never had.

She finished her cigarette and, whether by carelessness or malice, flicked the fag-end straight into the hole in front of him.

'Oi!' Jason said,

'What?' but he didn't know if she was pretending.

'You flicked your goddamn butt into the hole.'

'What? No I didn't.'

'What?' he was confused by such blatant denial. 'It's right here!'

'Bullshit, I tossed it into the bush, you must've dug one up or something.' It was in the hole, still smoking.

'Buggered if I'm gonna pick it up.' He

walked over to her, the shovel seemed stuck to his hand. 'Show some respect or something.' He was standing over her. She stood up and looked at him.

'Kiss me,' she said.

'What the f—'

But she didn't ask a second time. Instead she pressed her body against him like the weight of three years' of teen magazines on a shelf. Lips pushed together. Jason kissed her. He kissed her because he was sad and bored and if he let himself think on it, that equated to loneliness. He kissed her because there was dead dog on his fingertips and blisters hot but not yet formed. He kissed her because he knew he wasn't going to get paid for this and despite new-leaf bullshit part of him still wanted to take something back. He didn't know why she kissed him. But she was first to pull away. Smoke still on his breath he watched as she looked down, brushed dirt off her jeans and sat back down on the log, facing away from him. Jason shrugged, looked at her bra strap showing through and went back to the hole. When he next turned around she had gone.

He'd thought the hole had been finished. It was about knee deep. With a cross over it and a bit of luck, hopefully no kids would be digging it up soon. He'd put the cigarette butt over to the side so it didn't get mixed back in when he was filling the hole. He hated stuff like that and couldn't understand why she'd done it. But then he remembered the kiss and realised there was a lot of things he didn't understand about her. He'd turned around, perhaps to say something, but the sight of her absence made him forget.

He walked over to the log and stood there for a while, wondering if he should call out. In the end, because of the darkness or the distance, he didn't. He searched absentmindedly for a stick or something to make into a marker, but realised he was looking at head height, and for a girl. There'd be nothing to tie it together with anyway. He broke a few branches across his knee and then went to call out again, remembered she hated her name, coughed, said nothing.

The dirt wasn't coming out of his nails. He was walking back along the roadside, wiping his palms on his jeans and trying to not look suspicious. As a teenage guy, he'd found it was almost impossible not to look dodgy. He could tell this by the way police cars always slowed down when they passed, as if just wanting to be near him. It was proper dark now, and he had that nervous/sick feeling he got whenever he was walking to the school bus stop on a day of a test he hadn't studied for. Why the hell would she just walk off like that? He could already imagine what the gossiping café mothers would say. They'd probably judge him even worse than when Rozko tagged the side of the IGA. Every few metres he almost turned to go back. The walk home seemed longer, and he had to keep changing the hand he was carrying the shovel with. He was for sure going to get blisters. And probably arrested, if she wasn't home by the time he got there.

What if he just didn't go round? Sure they knew where he lived, but he could at least give it some time. Maybe just a couple more hours before they really started worrying, and in that time, perhaps she'd just go home. He wondered if she had a history of this kinda crap— he used to sneak out all the time. If that was the case maybe her mother wouldn't even be worried, just exasperated. But then he didn't want her to think that he'd just taken her daughter for a screw in the park. He kicked rocks as he walked, wondered if all the new leaves that he'd tried turning could just be given over to a forest fire. Did she even *like* him? Her face when she'd gone to kiss him could have been anything. He started dragging the shovel, enjoyed the noise it made and how it cut up the dirt like a snake following him home, and then he realised it could be evidence. Putting it back over his shoulders, which felt like hot knots. It was alright. Everything would be alright. He rubbed stones out from his neck. The hand that wasn't carrying the shovel felt empty. As he approached their crappy series of units he realised he still had nothing to say. The lights of the houses were blazing.

GUY SALVIDGE
Joe O'Sullivan Writers' Prize

THE CENTRE CANNOT HOLD

William is driving along a stretch of the Great Southern Highway near York. It's a misty winter's morning, the Getz' puny headlights a weak lamp upon a canvas of grey. An illusion of safety, a pocket of warmth. A soap bubble, an egg shell, a heartbeat.

Back it on up and you start again, Tim Rogers croons. *You start again.*

The song is over, last track on the CD, and now he wrangles it back into its jewel case, hunching forward to crack the glovebox open with his left hand while the right charts a course, while his attention is distracted by the burgeoning and burdensome—burgeonsome— souls pressed on polycarbonate plastic. Selecting one at random, driver's side wheels encroaching on the double white lines with a *thunk thunk thunk*, he turns his attention to the sharp curve ahead.

William is starting again, or trying to, and this necessitates a drive of more than one hundred kilometres to the Fremantle Arts Centre, where today he is enrolled in a creative writing workshop, his first in more than a year. On rare occasions, he makes the effort to re-surface from his obscurity and silence, but for the most part his debilitating pride is such that he cannot simply enrol in workshops and then attend them.

Oblivion lingers nearby, just a sharp turn to the left or right. He often consoles himself with the thought of writer Mikhail Bulgakov, hounded and blacklisted for his unacceptably bourgeois politics in Soviet Russia. Bulgakov somehow had the strength of character to write to Stalin asking to be deported, at a time when hundreds of thousands were disappearing into police stations, never to be seen again. Bulgakov died in 1940, shortly before the war with Germany, but not in the gulag.

Like Woody Guthrie on the stereo, William's had some hard travelin'. His marriage of ten years busted up a while back, he's stuck in a shitty job teaching dropkicks where to put capital letters and full stops at the local high school, and now a disc in his back has popped a hernia. He has no ambitions or interests beyond reading and writing, no friends outside work, no mentors aside from long dead writers. He drinks too much and exercises too little. He doesn't have a girlfriend.

When he arrives in Fremantle, there are a couple of spaces in front of the Arts Centre and he takes this as a sign of slender encouragement. He doesn't want to go upstairs to the workshop just yet or he might have to chat with someone, possibly even another writer, so he orders a coffee, sits in the corner of the café and makes sure to avoid eye contact.

By the time he makes it upstairs, the workshop has started. He sits down at a paint-flecked desk and gets out his journal and pen. It isn't the fault of the presenter, a rakish woman of about sixty, but the words wash over him. He imagines himself a literary black hole, where words pour in but can never again escape the terrible gravity. The woman stops speaking and the participants start scribbling in their notebooks or tapping on their laptops. So as not to attract attention, William writes:

> *Once upon a time and a very good time it was there was a moocow coming down along the road and this moocow that was coming down along the road met a nicens*
> > *little boy named baby tuckoo.*

It isn't even his; it's the opening to James Joyce's *A Portrait of the Artist as a Young Man*.

During the break, William grabs his tote bag and shuffles downstairs.

'How are you enjoying it?' a voice says. William startles not only in hearing the words but in perceiving that the question is intended for him. He looks at the speaker: a dark-haired woman of perhaps Middle-Eastern descent, his age or a little younger.

'Yeah, I'm …' he stammers. 'It's fine.'

'Mind if I sit with you? It's nice out here in the sun.'

'True.'

'I'm Alma,' she says, extending her hand. It's warm.

'William.'

'Pleased to meet you, William. What do you write?'

Write? 'Um, not enough.'

Her hair is wavy and tousled and she's wearing a black jumper. 'Me neither. But I'm trying, you know?'

William knows; he's nodding. He can feel a coil, an invisible rope, connecting them. 'I liked your bit about . . .' She spoke, didn't she? Read her work aloud. 'About your health issue.'

Alma exhales. 'It's embarrassing, but it's all I can think about.'

He's nodding again. All she can think about. A cyst on her ovary. 'So, you're having surgery?'

These are the magic words: out it pours. She'd been having abdominal pains, bloating. Then ultrasounds, blood tests, an expensive specialist appointment. It's her left ovary, the cyst swollen up to the size of a tennis ball, two centimetres bigger this month than last. If it's cancerous, she'll lose the ovary. Her operation is set for this coming Wednesday and, despite having private health insurance, it's going to cost her twelve hundred dollars.

'It must be hard going to the

ultrasound place when you're not, you know, pregnant.'

She bites her lip. 'Look, let's just get out of here, okay?'

'Where to?'

'I was thinking the casino.'

The casino? The only time he's been there was for an English teachers' conference, and he didn't do any gambling. Didn't learn anything either. 'I don't have much money.'

'Think I do? I need to raise the cash for my op.'

'Next you're going to tell me you have a system.'

'I do have a system.'

They climb into the Getz and get a clear run of green lights on the Canning Highway, which he interprets as a positive sign. The moment they step across the threshold of the casino, William finds himself being tailed by a security guard. 'You look like maybe you want to sign up for membership,' the guard says. He's talking to William, not Alma.

'How do you know I'm new?'

'Call it a hunch.' The guard ushers over a pair of casino employees wielding iPads and they sign him up. The women give him a rewards card and a voucher for a free drink.

'The bar's over there,' Alma tells him when the women are gone. 'I'll be back in a minute.'

The barman takes the voucher and pours William a glass of the house red. William asks the barman to break a fifty.

'Can't do that, regulations.'

'Fair enough. What's the cheapest thing on the menu?'

This is a better tack. 'A tomato sauce will cost you twenty cents.'

'Then I'll have a tomato sauce.'

'That's lunch sorted,' Alma says when she gets back from the toilet. She wants to play the pokies, so he watches her for a while.

'So, what's the system?' he asks.

'Keep pressing this button until I win.'

At a dollar a pop, it doesn't take her more than twenty minutes to lose fifty. She wins a bit here and there, but it all goes back. She particularly likes a machine that depicts a graveyard, the point being to get a board full of gravestones. He gets them another wine and now she's half way to losing another fifty.

'Maybe bet a smaller amount each time?' he says.

'How many stories have you sent out this year, Will?' she asks. The two topics don't seem related.

'I'm sorry?'

She doesn't take her eye from the screen or her finger from the button. A monkey could do the job just as effectively. 'You want to get a story published, don't you? How many have you sent out?'

He thinks about it. 'Um, one.'

'And how many times did you send it?'

He can see where she's going with this. 'I think twice.'

'I see. And how many competitions have you entered?'

'I entered the Margaret River competition. Didn't get anywhere.'

'So that's one.' She's down to twelve dollars from her original hundred.

'You think I should come to the casino more often, is that it?'

She flashes him a grin between rolls. Eight dollars left. 'Some competitions cost money, so it's like gambling. Pay fifteen bucks for the entry fee, probably get nowhere. Occasionally you win something, just like this.' She's won twenty dollars. 'I got second prize in that Peter Cowan prize a couple of years back. A hundred bucks, it paid.'

'Well, congrats.'

'Yeah, and I just lost a hundred bucks in half an hour, didn't I? I guess I thought I might win the twelve hundred I need. But life is about gambling, isn't it? You could have stayed at the workshop, but you thought you might get a root, didn't you? Busted ovary and all. Still might.'

Alma hits the button with her final dollar, but the stars won't align. She's reaching for her wallet.

He puts his hand over hers. 'My turn. Here, take a twenty and go get us another wine.'

'Right-o, Casanova.'

William loads twenty dollars onto his card and turns his attention to the game. If he bets a dollar per round, he'll be out before she gets back from the bar, so he makes it fifty cents. No skill, no choice, just whack. He loses twenty times in a row. After a while, he can't even be bothered looking at the screen anymore.

Alma gets back with their drinks and hands him a few dollars in change. 'Don't bet fifty, cheap ass, bet a dollar.'

He humours her, but stuffs up and ends up betting three dollars instead of one. Now he's down to five. He hits the

button again and the screen half fills with gravestones. Then the board re-rolls the other squares and most of them flick over to gravestones too.

'Shiiiit!' she says. The game draws a fence around the gravestones.

A fucking big fence.

WIN: $632.50, the screen says.

'Quick, press *Collect*.'

The machine spits out a paper ticket and Alma shows him where to exchange it for a wad of crisp fifties. He takes thirty bucks for himself and hands her the rest. 'Let's get out of here while we still can,' he says.

'But I need the other six hundred!'

'Just listen to yourself, would you? We walked in here an hour ago and now you're walking out with six hundred bucks.'

'I guess you're right. That root's looking like a slam dunk, isn't it?'

He gets behind the wheel—three wines won't kill him—and she sits there clutching her fifties. It's kind of sad, seeing her this happy. Turns out she lives in North Fremantle, practically around the corner from the Arts Centre. Now the rain's coming down and he's worse for wear on account on the wine.

'This is it,' she says, pointing to a non-descript brick and tile. He's tired and he has a long drive ahead of him. She gets out and opens the front door, then notices that he's still behind the wheel. 'What's your problem, stage fright? You won't hurt me.'

'It's not that.'

'I thought we were going to have a thing together. Maybe a big thing, maybe a small thing, who knows?'

'I like you, Alma. I just don't know.'

'I don't know if I'm going to be alive this time next week, do I? Maybe I'll bleed out on the table or die from an infection after the op. Maybe you'll get yourself killed driving home in that little matchbox. It's like the pokies, like sending out those stories. You've got to risk it.'

William gets out of the car and follows her into the house. In his mind's eye, he can still see a field of cartoon gravestones ringed by a cartoon fence.

MARK O'FLYNN
Leon Shann Melbourne Poets Union International Poetry Award

KITE

Remember. The past is gone for the moment.
Take hold of this string, its umbilicus of knots,
let your kite out slowly beyond the power lines
shaking off the starlings as you go.

Wait. There is nothing you can do. The wind
will not dry your shirts any faster if you
look away. The kettle will not boil, the custard
not set, the lava in your blood not cool.

Look. Here is my tea cup. There is your spoon.
The music of our little whirlpool.
My fork, your knife. Montague and Capulet.
Tintinnabulation of swords.

Give me shelter, or something, the lyrics of the old
songs go. Wipe the fever from my brow
with a handkerchief of cash. It's a false dichotomy
to think the sky belongs to any one of us.

Get out of the pool! the parrots cry in panic
at the coming storm. Clouds gather in doubt
like old scones, green with the gall of snow,
the chlorine catching at your throat.

Tempted? It won't take long to drink that glass of water.
Perhaps you'd like a straw, a desert to suck it up in
like a camel? Perhaps it won't even slake
your thirst. Perhaps only blood will.

Turn yourself inside out. That way we can see
whether or not you've eaten your greens. Not a pretty
sight, but like the violence of the big fish eating the little
fish, that's life, and at least someone is happy.

Consider. There on the street, an abandoned doll.
A doll with hair pulled out by the roots. One
eye missing. The last thing it saw plain in the expression
on its face. Perhaps not a doll at all. Perhaps a child.

In the china shop. Plates. Saucers. Gravy boats.
All that fine porcelain. The lathered bull,
banderillas dangling from his back, horns dripping,
weighing up his options. Who's next?

On my hot tin roof nine cats living one musical life:
a tortoiseshell, a tabby, a Persian, a Siamese,
a Sphinx, an Abyssinian, a Scottish Fold, a Liger,
a Manx without his rudder or, indeed, the attitude.

Here is a brick. Here another. Between them
a slice of cement like the filling in a cream biscuit
squeezed between the vertebrae. Another achievement
of age. In this fashion your tomb is well constructed.

FIGUE

my father's favourite fruit was a fig
and, like a fig,
my father flowered on the inside

Wagin, 1947, salt lakes and Salmon Gums,
post-war frugality, dance hall, my father the
vamping pianist, railway town, Baptist tracks rattling

fig, from the French 'figue',
a soft pear-shaped, many-seeded fruit

clattering atop keys, my father's hands, all the blacks,
not knowing how, the band,
paid in riders, post-gig drinks

dun brown the fig or a bruised purple,
call it petulant, or shy

sly kinship, the held look, man lingers
over man, my father, call it ekphrastic,
phrases hungering for another's art

fruiting twice each season, 'breva',
the first crop, on woody stems

my father, Baptist tracks clattering

flowering on the inside

AVRIL BRADLEY
Poetica Christi Press Poetry Competition. 2017 Theme: 'Wonderment'

FLIGHT OF THE MONARCHS

In heaven there is no loss or accident.
Everything knows its way.

(West African saying)

Miguel protects the forest in Sierra Chincua
for the milkweed butterflies' arrival.

Their slow, deliberate flight carries them
two thousand miles. The cold weather

ticks them off: says. 'Go'. 'Migrate.'
More than a millennia this has been so.

One hundred million North American monarchs,
each one weighing less than a cent,

glide en masse with slow, easy accuracy,
carried forward by their looping trajectories,

flimsy wings etched like leadlight windows
in a cathedral tower stretched over blue sky.

None of them ever know the way.
Yet, together they arrive each year on the Day of the Dead

revered souls returning to honour relatives
in night time vigil. Food and drink left for the dead to find.

Masses of marigolds strewn about and woven into crosses
reflect traceries of brown and gold butterfly colours.

Each soul   each monarch   each tree   precious
in the forest Miguel preserves as sanctuary.

MIRANDA TETLOW

Northern Territory Literary Awards – ZipPrint Short Story Award

THIS IS WHERE YOU COME FROM

I can still see the thin, white membrane ringed with blood. The calf inside, pushing against it, like someone very much alive and surprised to find themselves in a body bag. Grandpa was bending over the newborn in his work trousers, the ones with a fly permanently at half-mast. ('Peter! Those pants are for the bin!', Granny would have said back at the house) He ran his thumbnail along the filmy sheath until it popped, spewing out liquid the colour of rust.

I was sitting in the passenger seat of Grandpa's Subaru, tracing flowers into a layer of bull dust on the dashboard. Earlier, I had been allowed to drive the unregistered car from his lap, steering while he rode the clutch, the Subaru lurching along the dirt road that led from the homestead to the paddocks. Grandpa said he was taking me out for a treat. I was hoping for an icy pole from the workshop freezer, lemonade-flavoured and coated in a layer of icicles.

Had I known this was the treat, I would have stayed back at the house with Granny. From between my hands, I watched the calf unfold, sticky in her coat, not yet ready for those legs. Grandpa called out to me. I gripped onto my unused seatbelt. The cow started to lick her baby clean. Grandpa opened the car door and I made my body arch and stiffen.

He growled, 'Come on, Tilly! Be a big girl!'

I buried my face in the vinyl. Grandpa returned to his poddy calf and her mother, all teats and udder.

That story can't be entirely true, because I was only three years old at the time but that's how I remember it. Looking back now, what surprises me most is that the cow didn't make a sound. None of the deep-throated bellows you might have expected, the bovine version of expletives you'd hear in a fourth-floor maternity ward.

But then, I didn't make a sound either when my son was born. In my early labour, I could hear a woman in the neighbouring birth suite screaming for it to be over.

'Get. This. Fuckin'. Baby. The fuck. Out of me!'

'Don't worry,' the midwife assured me.

'Her baby's twice the size of yours and she's had no pain relief.'

I had all of the pain relief. Eventually, they extracted my son with a pair of forceps. They looked like salad servers, long and silver. He came out in a slither, all arms and legs, perfect apart from a slight indentation on his left ear.

Six weeks later, we went to visit Grandpa. He wasn't out in the paddocks anymore. The farm where I grew up was sold after Granny died, all 1600 acres of it swapped for a house in one of Canberra's nicest suburbs. Grandpa sat perched on a wicker chair. We presented him with our baby.

'Who have we got here, then?'

'This is Mischa,' I said.

'What is he—a Russian?' Grandpa beckoned me closer. 'You know I've already got a great-granddaughter named Poet?'

He shook his head.

'Poet. You don't get around in the playground much with a name like that.'

Grandpa inspected my son like he might have checked a horse at an auction. He held him up to the light; he examined his eyes, then his gums for teeth (there were none); he counted out fingers and toes. Grandpa ran his hands down Mischa's limbs, over the folds of skin that fell from shoulder to wrist and thigh to ankle like strings of party sausage rolls. He fingered the clip on his ear left by the forceps, a flaw that would have let him bargain price with the horse's owner, or with us, if we were in the business of selling our baby and he was in the business of buying one.

Then he harrumphed. 'Very good. You can take him back now.'

We were living in Darwin then. My husband Steve and I bought a small home in the northern suburbs, an elevated prefab with a tropical jungle out the back. Frangipani trees, vines that stretched between the palms, and a series of empty pots that served mostly to breed green tree frogs. Mischa learned to crawl, then walk in that garden. He celebrated his first birthday by swirling his hands in the stagnant puddles of mosquito larvae and frog spawn, licking his fingers clean.

One day, I got a phone call from Grandpa out of the blue. I held the phone away from my ear as he trumpeted an imminent arrival.

'Tilly? What are you doing next week?'

Darwin Airport smelled like wet wool and old dogs. I nursed my cup of coffee in the foyer while Mischa examined a luggage trolley, spinning the wheels with toddler intensity. Grandpa was easy to pick out in the crowd: tweed jacket, glasses fogged up. He crossed a stream of lily pads, the lotus flowers embroidered onto a heavy carpet that hadn't been updated in over a decade. When we hugged, my face pressed against his and I could feel the new slack of his cheek against mine. He rubbed my hands.

'How's my Tilly? And the little man?'

Grandpa chucked Mischa under the chin. He gestured towards the luggage carousel, and we walked over to collect his suitcase.

'If I'd known it was your wet season, I wouldn't have come,' he said. 'Some big storms on the way up. Pilot nearly had to land at Tindal but he pushed through. Good man.'

I reached over for his paper. In Darwin, we didn't get the interstate newspapers until mid-afternoon. It was something I missed. Spilling over the front page was a shock of red hair, and the blue and red lightning struck face of Ziggy Stardust.

'That picture's all over the papers,' he said. 'Some pop star.'

'David Bowie,' I said, grabbing his newspaper.

'Never heard of him.'

I rolled my eyes. 'Let's go,' I said. 'I'll take you the scenic way home.'

We drove back to our place in silence. It was low tide. Lonely mangrove trees poked out of the mud flats. Grey clouds pushed down on the horizon until the sea started to dissolve. Through the windscreen wipers, I spied two men walking along the bike path, bare chested and beaded with rain. They were holding magpie geese by the neck like they were umbrellas.

Grandpa rubbed his eyes. 'When are you going to come home? You're living on the frontier here.'

We pulled into the driveway, and I opened the gate, creaky with a padlock that was for show rather than security. I showed him around the house. He tried to hide his dismay at the guest bedroom, the low slung double bed and the click-click-click of the ceiling fan. Grandpa rested his suitcase on the dresser. I watched him run a hand along the bed, smoothing the sheets. They were already damp.

When Steve got home from work, we sat down to dinner. Mischa gurgled away in his high chair, flinging portions of potato salad onto the verandah. Within minutes, the mayonnaise started to curdle. There was a burst of lightning and the frogs answered in kind, a wet call and response.

A scream cut through the darkness.

I stood up straight away. 'What was that?'

'I'm sure it's nothing to worry about,' said Steve. He smiled wanly at Grandpa. 'Just some kid who doesn't want to go to bed.'

'What about that couple down the street? Should we call the cops?'

'Don't be ridiculous,' said Grandpa. He sat up as straight as our flimsy outdoor furniture would allow. 'Don't you two know anything about birds?'

We didn't.

I had friends who could point out a dot in the sky and a speck on a branch. *Whistling kite* and *sacred kingfisher* and *tawny frogmouth*, they could recite with a certainty and confidence about their place in the world. That wasn't me.

Grandpa nodded. 'Bush stone-curlews. There's probably a nest of them nearby. We'll have a look tomorrow.'

I scraped our plates into the bin, and called it a night.

In the morning, the rain was gone. Mischa was playing with his trike under the house and I hunted around for breakfast supplies. Grandpa was a firm believer in bacon and eggs. Instead, I held up a box of cereal like I was a hostess on a game show.

'Can I tempt you?'

He waved me away. 'Not right now, Tilly. Mischa and I are off to find the curlews! Aren't we, Mish? I'd reckon that nest is around here somewhere.'

Mischa pointed toward the sky. 'Bird!'

Grandpa clapped his hands. 'That's right! Bird! Come on, Mischa boy!'

I went back into the kitchen. Yesterday's paper was still sitting on the bench, and I stared at Ziggy Stardust. I thought about the parallel universe that Grandpa occupied in the seventies and eighties, the one devoid of David Bowie. The surgery where he treated hayfever and chronic allergies. The tennis afternoons, the rounds of golf. The dam we used to swim in when the temperature hit forty degrees, mud flaking off us afterwards like plaster of Paris. The dinner parties on the verandah. The back paddock, filled with cow pats and granite boulders.

That was my universe, too. How did Bowie even find me?

My friend Katrina's seventh birthday. Her lounge room, transformed into a blue light disco, with her older brother Marty in charge of the stereo. He liked The Clash, Michael Jackson, The Sex Pistols. It was not a parentally endorsed set list. Then Marty pulled out a new cassette tape. He slotted it into the deck with a snap and pressed play.

That's when I heard Bowie for the first time.

*There's a brand new dance
but I don't know its name…*

I remember being thrilled by that Bowie bass line, by the dirty glamour of it all. We strutted through the lounge room. We turned to the left. Fashion! I begged Marty to rewind the tape, to play it again. From then on, Bowie and his cast of characters would drip feed into my life. The Jean Genie. Ziggy. The Goblin King. Major Tom. Through his multi-coloured eyes, I saw the world projected on a screen bigger than ours, with edges that were blurry, darker, more interesting.

I put the newspaper and Bowie's vacant face back down on the bench. I heard a smack. The braking of wheels on the bitumen. And then a scream, and this time it wasn't a fucking curlew.

We had steps leading down to the drive way, but my feet didn't feel them. Maybe I flew.

A car had stopped and a stranger was on his phone, gesticulating wildly. And there he was.

On the road, a splay of limbs in a puddle that was thick and dark. I flapped my wings again. Circled above and then landed. He wasn't moving. If he was breathing, I couldn't feel it. I pressed my hands into the ashvalt so hard my skin broke. People were talking to me and then they stopped, because I started making sounds the cow never did when she gave birth to that body bag with the calf inside.

When I opened my eyes, I could just make out three paramedics in high vis. There were a couple of police officers and a man who kept apologising, sweat dribbling over his top lip. I closed them again. At the hospital, someone put a cup of tea in my hands. It was from the staff room, rather than the cafeteria, a pixelated photo of someone's cat was printed along the outside.

Grandpa slumped in the chair beside me.

'Tilly.'

I stared at him.

'I just, I'm just … I'm so very sorry.'

Grandpa's face was white underneath the fluorescent lights.

'It should have been you.'

He looked at me, broken. I bit down hard on the cat mug; I said it again.

Grandpa got up from his chair. He muttered something about the vending machine, getting something to eat.

They let us into the room where Mischa was lying still on the bed. The doctors said we could stay with him. Steve fell asleep in the chair; I lay awake on the floor, refusing the pillows and blanket the nurse offered me. I shivered all night in the hospital's overzealous air-conditioning.

When I went home to pick up some things, Grandpa was long gone. No note. Just the outline of his suitcase in the dust I hadn't cleaned off the dresser, his razer left behind in the bathroom like an angry calling card, though I knew he'd just forgotten it. I picked it up. There were stray whiskers left in the blunt blades. I ran my fingertips over them until the skin broke again.

There were weeks of scans and second opinions. A broken leg, a fractured wrist, the rest we couldn't be sure of. Not yet. Mischa abandoned the few words he had at his disposal: No, Dada, Mama. Bird. There. They disappeared along with the wet season. I traced the scars on his head every night, like lines on a map.

In the right light, I could still see a Mischa-shaped stain on the road. I tried to erase it with the wheels of our car, driving between our house and the hospital.

Finally, I saw them. The curlews. The mother stood like a statue in the garden. She loomed over her hatchling, its feathers grey and charcoal, soft and smudged. She jutted her head forward, raising her scalloped wings like a shield when we got too close.

'Look, Mischa!' I said. 'Bird!'

He smiled back at me.

It should have been you. The words were still rolling around my mouth like a hard toffee. I thought about calling to apologise. I didn't.

Someone called me instead. My Aunt Helen. Grandpa was in hospital.

When we arrived, Grandpa's face was waxy. His breath was slow on the inhalation, scratchy and rattling on the exhalation. I sat down on the edge of his bed, and the springs almost gave way.

'We need to talk about end of life care,' the doctor told me.

On the first day, I sat there holding his hand. Steve and Helen took Mischa to the gift shop to pick out a balloon. I stared at the print above Grandpa's bed. A man stood at the edge of a shearing shed verandah, his eyes vacant. Waiting.

On the second day, Grandpa opened his eyes once and did a roll call. Tilly, Steve, Mischa. Helen. Pamela and Bob. He numbered us off and went back to sleep.

On the third day, he was awake when I walked in with an orange juice from the cafeteria. He asked me what day it was. 'Thursday,' I said. Mischa was eyeing off the chocolates on the side table. 'Do you remember Mish?'

'Of course I remember Mischa.' Grandpa snorted. We talked for a few moments, then he pressed his face back into the pillow and raised a hand to dismiss me.

But a week later, he was sitting up in bed. It was almost Christmas and the nurses made half-hearted attempts at festivity. An artificial tree wrapped in tinsel sat on top of the television. Next to it, a small, plastic Santa that rocked back and forth when you put it under a light.

'I don't think much of that masturbating Santa,' he said, and I thought he was coming back to us.

It was around that time that I remembered the birth of the poddy calf, all those years ago.

'Yes,' he said. 'That's right. Your mum was in the hospital; we were looking after you. You wanted to call the calf Baby David.'

After my brother. That piece of the story was lost in the ripping membrane, the shaky calf covered in blood, the childhood tantrum. Because David never came back from the hospital. Mum left home two months later. She said she was driving to Cairns to figure things out, though we heard later that she didn't get further than Pennant Hills.

It should have been you. As if I could have exchanged Grandpa for Mischa. Swapped the poddy calf for David.

Stopped Mum. No. Death stands on a lazy susan in a busy restaurant and spins. You. Not you, but you.

When I arrived at Grandpa's house, after his funeral, my aunts had already picked it over for valuables. Just the flotsam of my childhood remained. Old tennis rackets. Cupboards bursting with crockery, drawers filled with mismatched cutlery. There was a copy of the Karma Sutra and a jar of dried salad herbs from the eighties, judging by the font and peeling label. In one of the wardrobes, I found my old CD soundtrack to *Dawson's Creek* and a chess set painted up like the family of the last Russian Tsar.

A jumble of vinyl sat next to the old record player. I flicked through the covers. Tchaikovsky, Verdi, Vivaldi. The Very Best of the London Symphony Orchestra. No Bowie, of course, but Grandpa had his own space oddities. I was about to lock the door behind me when I saw one of Mum's old toys, still sitting on the shelf. A silver bird that balanced on a nail by its beak, wings outstretched. Mum showed it to me when she was pregnant. She tapped on the bird's rump and it bobbed up and down, cradled mid-air by physics, an invisible thread, and the universe. I left everything else behind, but I took the bird home for Mischa.

RACHAEL MEAD
2017 NALAG Grieve Poetry Prize

POWERLESS

Three days without power and the only sounds
are wind, rain and the hiss of flame beneath the kettle.

I don't mind. Quiet is the road blocked by tree-fall,
reminding us that electricity is not the fifth element.

I am reading on the couch when our neighbour
knocks.   *Tom has died*, she says.

It's the final erasure of that disease, the one
that eventually steals everything, from his last

conversation to the memory of his wife of 60 years.
She is strong but after she leaves the grey air

seems especially sad and even a little jagged.
The world is not what we want. Our minds,

those tender, playful muscles stiffen and seize,
however hard we work at making ourselves

original. Beyond the glass, the green earth
blurs with rain, the trees bend and crack

in allegories of wind.   My heart folds
and folds itself down into a tiny yet infinitely

dense thing: a grain of sand, a mote of dust,
a faraway star we know full well is dead.

UNSPOOLING

This is what your shirt felt like under your hand while you lay on the hospital bed. The shirt was dark blue, cheap cotton from Target that you no longer wear. You worked five fingers into your breastbone, touching something solid. Here are the two words the nice doctor gave, out of all the words, that made you cry the most: one was *cervix*, the other was *dilate*. Those words wanted to sink you. But you remained on the surface, floating near the pair of medical students who stood, suddenly silent, somewhere at the end of the bed. The probe was slick and cold inside you.

Afterwards, you saw a woman smoking outside the front of the hospital, a tight white singlet stretched across her belly. Seven? Eight months?

There was your breathless rage. There was your boyfriend, Joe, at your elbow, guiding you past.

This is how it felt, to hear there was no longer a heartbeat.

This is the letter the government department has sent Joe, advising him that he could be deported. Here is the number of days until he might go: twenty-eight. A number as small and square and bureaucratic as the postage stamp on the envelope. Here is the lawyer's website. This is the figure the lawyer quoted to help save him and it's astronomical, eye-watering, but also doable. Essential.

This is the title of the visa Joe must apply for: *Remaining Relative (subclass 835)*. Don't blame yourself—you didn't know. He came to this country young. He went to school here—a place in Sydney (nicer than where you went, as though that makes a difference). A photograph shows him among two dozen other beefy, gleaming lads in red jumpers. In the front row of the photo is the classmate who shortened his name to *Joe*. A name easier to pronounce than the one he was given, a name that stuck.

You met the classmate and his wife when the four of you shared plates of Spanish food by the river, the *calamares fritos* and *patatas bravas*. Joe loves this couple. There was an eagerness to please them that you didn't entirely like, but he seemed to glow, so you played your part to win them over. Nobody at tapas knew about that word, visa. Under the restaurant table you and Joe were palm to palm, electric-stroking, a squall of joy at your throat. You didn't touch the sangria, and what a waste that turned out to be.

Here are the terms of the payment plan. The email from the lawyer seems generous and methodical, merely pointing out, not embarrassed (like you would be) to be quoting individual payment installments as though they were the total sum. Don't blame him. All this time Joe was wrapped in this invisible problem. Quickly, you decide not to make it about you, about the betrayal you feel. Because it's all there in his letter from the government, and nothing in the letter mentions you.

He gives you such a look when you suggest maybe his home country isn't such a bad place to live. Like he could return. You suggest following him there for good. And you are so sorry for knowing nothing at all worth knowing about a country other than your own. He says flatly, 'Trust me.'

Don't recall it too often, do not dwell. But you knew the baby for such a short while. Something switched on in the dark, then switched off.

Remember your impatience, never grown out of? Something he noticed the first weekend you stayed at his place when all the avocadoes on his kitchen bench refused to ripen. Months later, the sum of all the food you could stomach was avocado on toast, salt-and-peppered and gobbled flat on your back on the couch. He came home from the markets and unpacked the brown paper bag, laughing and piling them into your hands.

Don't name it. Don't wonder about its sex. Don't send out for a handmade silver oval pendant half the size of a postage stamp to wear around your neck. Don't feel bad that you sprinted up a hill, in the cold, in the dark. Don't Google anything. Don't seek out that TV show you mainlined those few days to take your mind off what was happening. (Never again, even though, truth be told, it was a terrific show.) Don't look at the pale, soft things you bought to put in a bassinet. Don't forget your good posture. Don't forget your exercises. Keep it up.

Keep everything up.

Knife open the carton on your doorstep, pull the merlot or shiraz or whatever the fuck it is from its cardboard womb (don't say womb) and upend it into that big globe of a glass, that one, there. Joe says, 'Here, I'll hold it still.'

This was the dish he cooked the first night you stayed over. *I should make you something from home, but I'm bad at it*, he said, laughing, newly showered after work.

This is the difference between him and your ex. Between him and all the men you've dated. Here and here and here and that mountain up to the sky, so vast. As different as a bear and a fish. A moth and a gull. Also small things: he uses reflexive pronouns correctly and buys the good mandarins. He traces your inner thigh with his close-cut nails. He says *folks*. He says *love*. He breathes you in.

Don't forget that whole blazing life he had before you met him. (Doing his biology homework, clashing his head and shoulders into scrums, shipping himself off to Port Hedland for three years, visiting his sister in hospital and shifting his car from street to street so that he wouldn't get towed. Each time he returned to the psychiatric ward the nurse at the front desk asked if he was carrying any aluminium cans. Some patients sliced them into pieces that were sharp, his sister said.)

This is the name of the Minister. Here is his doughy, dull-eyed face. A threat like this feels like being shot, feels like being emptied. Empty, emptier, emptiest. Here is the Minister's website with its slideshow of photos (energised in parliament, aglow at a school awards night, hard-hatted at a roadside. Other pictures not shown: fingering a name on a database, approving a digital signature, folding the paper, licking a stamp).

*

Yesterday, you drove to the beach and took photos together. Time is slipping by: less than three weeks now. How silly you'll feel—how delicious it would be to feel silly—if this all amounts to nothing, these serious photos posed by the tall pines next to the sand. He checked his phone for messages. The lawyer's office said they would ring for a chat when a court date had been settled. The clerk wouldn't text that sort of thing.

When you got home from the beach, Joe sat at the dining table with a pencil and a sheet of A4 and scored lines down the page and then quick, heavy lines across. A grid. A calendar. He didn't share it with you but let you watch while he circled and shaded in boxes. These were the extra shifts he'd lined up with his boss to make that second payment. By then you'd peeled off your bathers and changed into his shirt and nothing else. He brushed the paper and the graphite streaked the back of his hand. He reached for you. He undid some buttons, saying, 'You're trying to be cute, I can tell.'

Your friend on the other side of the country has travelled the world far more than you. She points this out. She sends you a text message: *Don't be surprised if this is actually out of your control. You must prepare yourself*, she says, *for the worst.*

And this is not even the worst. You know it. So many people have it much, much worse. This is what you're supposed to say—that it is good and right to Have Some Perspective. But this pair of things, coming one then two, leaves you feeling bruised.

Here is the future you'd planned.

The two of you walk past protesters outside parliament on the way to the lawyer's office, seventeen days before the letter's end date. A man stands on the footpath calling for the dismantling of the police state. He is threatening to set things—nothing specific—alight. You're surprised how well dressed he is, how close to your own age. But is this okay, to be surprised? At least he's better than that other man, at least eighty years old in belted shorts and long white socks, who shields his chest with a photograph of a salmon-blushing foetus in utero and letters marked out in gaffer-tape that say, *This is not a potato.*

The lawyer understands your anguish. All your days now are numbered. Yes, they will ring you with a court date. He gets it. He's done this a hundred times, a thousand times and, please, have sympathy for him. Please pay him, too. It looks like a lot of money, but this is probably just what lawyers cost, even if you were to lose and Joe be forced to leave.

And don't ask questions about that. Like, who pays for the aeroplane ticket? Will he be shackled to the seat in front? Does he get fed? Will someone drape a blanket across his lap? Which country does he belong to in the placeless, starry, limbo-hours?

Remember how good your penmanship was as a girl, when you'd decide which of your friends might like to receive a letter? Your mother would pluck her address book from her handbag and read addresses aloud while you adored your pretty letters and numbers, your *4-6-5-0*. When those who replied sent their replies to your letterbox, you doubled over with excitement. 'Don't burst,' your mother said.

Waiting was the hardest part.

You could write to him, you could call. You could break it all off.

You could visit, you could move. Book a ticket, text your friend a message to say that it isn't brave to migrate there, not really. Pretend you're more in love than you are. Pretend you're less in love. No promises to yourself. No longer is there durability in anything, but the lawyer seems good and maybe you'll have a win this time.

Joe holds your hand stepping down from the kerb outside the office. You touch your belly. That kickback again. Dreadful again. There's nothing there. Find your pocket. Pocket your hand.

At home, later, you sit on the edge of the bath. He works his fingers into the back of your neck while you flex one foot against the vanity. You notice a mint green face washer, a new cake of soap, threads of orphaned hair near the drain in the floor. In the hours after your surgery you submerged only your feet in the bath water (*no swimming, no sex, no big life decisions*) and wondered at the neighbours in the flat next door. You could hear them taking apart their balcony doors, scraping the lead paint away. You imagined sex with Joe again, never thinking back then that the next time might be in his home country. On a beach, in a bare and tiny flat, beside a river. On your tiptoes, the way you like, hips tilted up. Your body strong and fit, recovered once more.

Print it off, tattoo it, write it in sharpie on every limb: *You don't get everything you want.* You would have told it to your baby. That parenting book about grit, that one about resilience, the one about teaching kindness and compassion. Would it have helped Joe to read a book

about going unnoticed? To fly under a
radar, so far below, that he emitted no
signal that reached Canberra? Don't
ask if he's done anything wrong. The
government's radar is broad, tentacular,
with no heartbeat. Don't unspool the
thread of your life together, here in this
country, before you've had it, or ever will.
Twenty-eight days. Eighteen days. Now
seventeen. Don't pretend you'll be able to
rein that in.

When his phone rings, his hand is in
your hair. You look up. He keeps his five
fingers on your scalp. The pressure is good.
He studies the screen. He smiles at you.

'Here we go,' he says.

ANOTHER GIG.

He can always hear a piano playing in his head when he looks through these glistening trees, a pavane, desolate in the silent and grieving countryside, the foliage sodden, secret, greenish-black. Discords sound in the car's thrum, the hooting wind forcing the chassis to swing and rattle, a blues rhythm now overriding that demure, ghostly old dance in his brain.

Up ahead the town shapes itself. A few small, stained cottages first, chimneys signalling with desperate little wisps, then a few sheds, then one or two buildings in grand Victorian smugness: bank, Town Hall, pub. More than one of those, of course. Tasmanian towns of more than two hundred can usually run to three or four.

'There's ours.' Alex, knuckle-knocking at the windscreen. Through the slapping wipers a rain-soused sheet of ruddy sandstone proclaims the face of The Empire. Another wash of grey water across the glass swabs it away.

Towns around here are miserable, trapped in dole and despair. The copper mines, the paper mills, the logging; they've poisoned, gouged, decapitated and then taken off. But lives, of course, don't. They stay, bilked and tight-lipped with outrage and when you think of it, grief.

'What a hole.' Alex again. The main street dribbles down his side window, runnels of black, brown and just occasionally a bright yellow; perhaps a kid wearing a safety mackintosh. No one moves for a few moments, revving up to leap from the dank warmth of the car and launch all the gear swiftly into the Lounge Bar. 'The place will pong of yesterday's vomit,' he declares in Glasgow vowels, 'and what's the bet they offer to pay in beer.'

'Tell me something new,' mutters Nick, saddle-sore and pocketing the car-keys.

These places all have crimson carpets with pompous patterns. Loud, blowsy roses, fleur-de-lis, unicorns, with booze, ash, and probably blood woven in. Underneath them, half the floor stumps would have caved in over the century so that walking down the hall or climbing the stairs makes you seasick.

And all, all, full of drunks.

Laughing drunks, like wounded galahs; crying drunks, usually for good reason; fighting drunks with too many head-punches notched up; gummy-mouthed, swearing drunks. And long after closing time, they bay in the street under your window.

The publican, he's typical too, a red-faced brawler, remaining hair in greasy clusters protecting each ear, nose a furious plum, aggression (at anything) on Simmer as he takes in the two musos, skivvy and jeans-clad. (*One of whom, for Chrissakes, is wearing specs.*)

'Where's the rest of yer?' His chin rises.

'We're it.' Nick takes in the clammy-faced aficionado.

'Rock. 'N metal. Right?'

'Blues. And harmonica. And Hawaiian slide.'

'Jesus.'

Disgust hisses out of a mouth-side, spluttering through teeth. 'The people they—look, fellas, there's some kinda—'

'No. there's not.' Alex, stepping forward, unfolds the booking slip. 'You signed for us, you got us.' He rubs it in, adding maliciously, 'We do a lot of our own material, too.'

Heaving with the effort at patience, Red-Face explains, hands splayed like hams along the slops-towel.

'Look, no offence. It's a rough pub, see. They like rough music. Y'know? Loud? With a beat. 'N a choon. Cold Chisel. Accadacca. That typa thing.' His eyes plead for compromise. Behind him a damp gaggle watches a race on the satellite TV clamped to the wall below the Queen's portrait. She seems to be checking out the dartboard on the opposite wall. Whatever, the patrons seem to be toasting her, glasses and eyes raised as they take in the Melbourne Trots.

'We'll work something out,' declare the boys, having no intention.

*

'Play "Highway to Hell", ya poofters!'

The crowd boils and seethes below the duo on the tiny stage. Swinging punches, flailing, roaring, guzzling. In rhythm. To songs of rude and sweaty love, of laborers, of heroes, Alex's harmonica sobbing of people who travel the rails for love or labor or cry out for loneliness, Nick's guitar strings plucking out the beat of the wheels, the tramp of poor feet as they trudge through a delta, a desert, a broken-down town, the drinkers down on the floor little realising it, but stomping the story out too. Is it my imagination, he wonders, or are there really no women down there? No, that couldn't be right, but that writhing, beery octopus competing with the rain that bashes on the roof above is distracting, it's impossible to see properly. And can't these yokels get it, he thinks, his fingers on auto-pilot, *these songs.* Black men in another country might have set them down, but these are songs of the men down there. Cries of fury, tribulation, yearning.

'How about "Runnin' Bear"!'

Christ, it's hopeless. *You should've been a teacher, like Mum said.*

'TIME!'

Hidden somewhere among the fusty plaster frills on the wall, a loudspeaker gargles into life, the battle entering its final phase.

The pub doors gape now into the soaking blackness, the one and only streetlight showing a thick dribble from holey guttering somewhere overhead. Shouldering through the cauldron of bodies, Red-Face and a few other heavies are on the march, selecting random staggering dancers and, using individual collar and belt as handles, hurling them out into the street. The swirling ejections are an obvious and regular message; most are now leaving, limping as if wounded.

'Finish up, fellas,' orders the rasping PA and the guys oblige with a tremolo of shuddering cadences.

Red-Face and his bouncers, bodies the size of caravans, move across the floor again, carrying lengths of chain thick as hawsers, weighted here and there with giant padlocks. Now they are launching them, looping them around and over fridges, cupboards, bar shelves, the chains landing like smashed plates, locked on and given a goodnight kick.

'Stops 'em thievin'.'

Red-Face again, explaining to Nick's gaping, un-mouthed query. He jerks his head at the windows, 'Like them.' (The windows are made of glass bricks.)

Suddenly a voice from out in the street, cultivated, almost professorial, shouts into the bar, into the din of the crashing chains.

'Nothing will come of nothing.'

Amazed and for some reason, appalled at the urbanity, the knowledge in that voice, here, in this place, Nick strains to see the speaker.

A man stands, back-lit in the pub doorway, hands on hips, a little light showing up the potential of a beer-gut and shiny scalp, all that can be deciphered in the glare from the streetlight and the wet black of the shadows.

'Misery loves company.'

The silhouette turns and flicks out of sight.

*

Oh, thank God, bed at last.

The room above the bar smells of damp earth and mothballs, the mattress feels as if stuffed with iron filings and the one narrow window is caked here and there with some unidentifiable muck. But the sheets are clean and the room is warm. Alex is almost asleep before Nick can pull his boots off. The night outside says *hush, whish, swoosh* with fluttering wind but for the most part it's silent, that kind of wild country silence that's almost frightening. As usual, Nick has what he calls a *big head* after playing, his eyes feel as if punched and swollen, no doubt from all the cigarette smoke and the clammy fug of too many unwashed bodies careening across a jam-packed floor. But soon, the wind outside soothes him to dozing, the occasional creak of bedsprings assures him it's time for rest and so he can relax and think and maybe even dream.

He tries not to admit to the panic that will assail him on nights like these, gigs like these, that sense of uselessness, it's gutting. Writing songs about lives that people couldn't give a shit about, what's he doing this for. But still he does. There's gentle tapping at his window now, in synch with the rhythm of of the wind, and the regularity of it means he can't get to sleep yet.

Standing at the window, he can just make out the tree, its twisting, tufted branches nudging timidly at the glass. King Billy pine, it's called, so tall it must be a hundred years old, he knows this from geography at school and it's way out of its comfort zone here.

Now why does this bring back to him that trip in America, that near-disaster when he stopped for petrol somewhere in Colorado and left his wallet on top of his car and drove off, way, way down the highway to the next gig and didn't realise what he'd done until he'd pulled in to the motel in Breckenridge. His fright at having lost every card, every piece of ID, every buck, meant a phone call to his sister in Melbourne in the middle of the night, and who promised to get to Western Union by the time it opened up next morning; money would be sent through, he was not to stress, all would turn out right.

And then the call on his mobile from a perfect stranger whose accent was so impenetrable Nick could hardly understand a word, asking his name, birthday, musicians' union card number. The perfect-stranger-truckie who arranged to deliver the wallet he'd found lying on the ground in the petrol station to him in the next town the very next day.

King Billy taps applause on the window and Nick begins to think of a new lyric for a melody that's been sitting on a tape in his studio back home.

*

The morning full of sputtering icicles, tearful barbed-wire fences stretching onwards, and in his sore head that piano *obbligato,* always mournful, ruminating.

Somewhere in these forests, miners once laid down rail-tracks to cart ore to the smelters, then abandoned them when the mines ran out. After a century, no-one remembered them, the forest's calm tyranny of vines and undergrowth devouring, keeping them secret.

Thinking of the tracks that lost their way, Nick remembers the end to that story, how a few years ago some poor lost bastard had fallen over in that wild place and landed on a rusted metal rail. Those tracks, found again.

He sighs, that piano playing in his head. But here is the sun, making an effort to polish the roadway and the soaked gravel. Off to Deloraine today.

****

KEVIN BONNETT
Cliff Green Short Story Competition

COOL AND WET TO THE TOUCH

Did you hear that? The blast? City express, on its way. Railway crossing in the distance. All melted, buckled tar, silver snake rails. Somehow still functional to metal monsters, grand gleam and fug on the blind corner. In the bright you could miss the flashing lights. If you want.

Let's give it a go. Make a run for it. Take a chance. Have a flutter, Russian roulette on the city express. Wallace would like the idea of me taking a punt. Having a bet.

Wallace kindly left the farm to me and the kids. Good of him. The weak chinned prick. Left a double mortgage, car loan, and tab at the service men's club; twelve fish and chips, six chicken parmas, fourteen schooners, three double scotches.

Pokies. Couldn't resist the pokies. Loved a flutter did Wallace. Thought he were in them ads, you know, impress the young fillies, high five his mates. Until it was time to pay the electric or gas, feed and haulage, heifers, lambs to the slaughter. The drought on us, all over us, again. Calling the contractor to gouge a ditch and bury carcasses. Months of fence fixing for invisible herds. All our final scrawny lambs sold up last spring. Who doesn't like spring lamb? Poor little mites.

He didn't seem to mind leaving the kids. No word on a weekend visit, a train out from the city to catch up with Cedric and Sheya. Shouldn't have given the poor lad that bogus name. Cedric. Destined to be a gardener or theatre critic. I've renamed him Tony. No more Cedric after his grandfather. On the land himself for seventy years until a double barrel got him. No suspicious circumstances, as they say. Look away. In the land, on the land, the land in him.

Wallace ran off to the big smoke. A bankrupt farmer's no worries in the city. No one knows. He's not on the computer, yet. Brown collar crime. Just has to be good with a crowbar or hauling bricks. Crumbling spine like his dad. Give him five years before the wheelchair.

If you look close he has pokie lights behind his eyes. Wallace can sing the little dinky Asian songs from memory winning fifty times twenty cents. Enough for the taxi home if he hadn't put it straight back into the silver tongue machines.

Obviously missed that maths class on probability. Missed most of school I'd say. Red dust drift through childhood, eyes firmly closed. Family, children under the blinds.

Can't do it on my own. I just left Tony and Sheya with mother for an hour. Call it respite if you like. But an hour's the limit. She's likely to put them in the oven with a lemon in their gobs. Evening roast with thyme and rosemary, legs out the door. I had a date with the bank. Mr shiny suit, soft hands, white-brite teeth, squinting at exponential, expansion debt numbers.

'Yes Mrs Turnbull, the loan is valid. Payments are still required.'

Payments are still required?

It's 43 degrees on the pavement and it hasn't rained for months. A double-D passes in the street, dust and grit spits the glass. On it's way to slaughter.

We're all on our way to slaughter. Bank slaughter. Looks in town slaughter. General store-tab-owing-slaughter. Little deaths.

My son, my daughter, are all I got left.

So we're coming around the bend to the crossing, back to farm, home, and this time I'm sure there'll be a padlock on the gate.

Again.

Now the red lights are clear and flashing. When nothing is for certain. It's only a question of continuing; when not much good has come from anything we're ever done. Family, farm, you name it. The shit sum of us.

I hear a sound but it's not the train, it's Tony.

'Ma, ma!' He screams. I glance, my foot flat punching the car, to beat the booms, beat the express, beat the banks.

His hand reaches out pointing, shaking, because he wants another chance, he knows and feels the dust and the sky. But more than anything he understands this particular sky. I blink. Jesus! A great roiling oily topped bank of rain drenched clouds fill the wind screen from top to bottom.

I wind the window down and judder to a halt, boom gates dancing, lights, bells and the rapid slush of the passing train mingles with dust and grit, and the dank stench of immanent rain.

The air con fan, click, click, clicks as Tony grins. He's a country kid who knows the meaning of rain. Things will be okay for now, even for a while at least, until next time.

The boom arms rise and we cross the rails and chase the corrugated ribbon to farm. When we get there the gate swings open easy with the wind. Cool and wet to the touch. Cool and wet to the touch.

SHELLEY HANSEN
2017 Open Award & Marian Mayne Trophy, CJ Dennis Poetry Competition

MY NAME'S DOREEN

'What-o!' he said. 'It's been a bonzer day.'
And then he said, 'How is it for a walk?'
How dare he try to chat me up that way!
That kind of talk
is for another sort of girl – not me –
and so I tossed my head to let him see.

My name's Doreen. I was a working girl
back then, and I remember how I cried
the day my life unravelled in a whirl
when father died
and left us debts. So all my hopes and plans
dissolved in never-ending rows of cans.

My father always said, 'Girl, you're no fool.'
And so I studied hard, and had a dream
that I'd become a teacher in a school –
but all the cream
was taken from that cake – it turned to ash
while working in a cannery for cash.

The larrikins would whistle us and stare
or try to sidle up and steal a kiss;
so when I saw him often standing there
I thought that this
was just another bloke who thought a flirt
was his just for the asking – and it hurt.

I knew his type. I'd heard the talk of fights
down Little Lonsdale Street, with broken bricks.
They gathered there on lamplit weekend nights
with fists and kicks
to settle, in the age-old way of men,
imagined scores – beyond a woman's ken.

I thought he'd go away and not return
or chase some other girl who'd play his game.
But his intentions, I was soon to learn,
were not the same
as others of his kind – when, in a while
he got us introduced in proper style.

We sat down by the beach. Bill held my hand
and talked. I hardly knew just what to think.
He said the moonlight in my eyes was grand!
It turned me pink
with blushes – then he made a solemn vow,
'I'll chuck the fighting clean,' he said, 'right now!'

I said I wished he meant it, but I knew
he meant it fair and square, there on that beach;
and though he'd lapse at times, still it was true.
His 'little peach'
he called me, but the cold hard light of day
soon brought me close to throwing it away.

I knew a bloke who wore a cute straw hat –
he gave me pretty flowers once or twice.
My thoughts for him were tuppence – less than that –
but it was nice
to have a treat. Yet it was plain to see
he loved his own reflection more than me.

That's when I found how much Bill really cared.
We had a row that nearly broke my heart,
and then I knew our love could not be shared.
It was the start –
a turning point, for better or for worse,
a brand new page, a chapter, and a verse.

Folks often ask me what I see in him –
a man of humble past, who talks quite rough.
They think my future prospects might be grim,
but it's enough
for me to see the love-light in his eyes –
the poetry that he cannot disguise.

'In sickness and in health' – we're side by side.
Our wedding day – with lifelong vows to take.
He looks at me with mingled hope and pride
as if I'll break –
and though I sweetly smile and play along,
he doesn't know I've never felt so strong!

The years – what will they bring? We cannot tell.
The world may share our joy or bring us pain
that must be faced – and yet I know full well
I won't complain
if all my days I'm blessed to share the yoke
of life with Bill – my Sentimental Bloke.

CASSIE HAMMER
Shoalhaven Literary Award

IN THE DEEP

Trinh adjusts her goggles. Doesn't bother to de-fog. The less she sees, the better. Through misty plastic, sea and sky are an endless, grey soup. White water swirls like soap scum at her feet.

I hate you, she whispers to the sea.

I hate you too, the sea whispers back.

She presses her goggles one last time and wades in. Diving under the first wave she feels strong. The second takes her breath. By the third she is gasping, and there is something else as well—an undercurrent that is coiled around her legs and dragging her into the deep.

Trinh's feet search for the sand in the way of an anchor seeking the sea bed but it refuses to come. As another wave breaks, the white water rushes her nose, eyes, ears and lungs. Her panic is lemonade, fizzing and spitting and fear runs like sugar in her veins. Roaring in her ears. The smell of diesel. Children screaming. Wood splintering. A past that is not hers. That she has no right to fear.

Trinh closes her eyes. Hears the voice of Coach Dunnett.

Chest up. Shoulders back. Eyes to the sky. Let the water hold you.

In this boiling ocean, backstroke is going to save her life. Her favourite. She knows enough not to swim against the current. Knows it will peter out, if she just lets it.

She kicks sideways and feels herself starting to float outside of her body, up into the mauve sky into which the moon is now rising. She sees herself as the seagulls do. Her white round face as a small moon, shining up at the bigger one above.

She gets it now. The trophies and ribbons that give her bedroom a carnival atmosphere mean nothing here. The pool is a puppy dog on her leash. The ocean is a monster that wants to swallow her whole.

After twenty minutes, she is back on the sand. Exhausted and shivering, she takes her towel to the boulders of the break wall, rocks that have spent their day doing nothing but soaking up the sun, and lets the radiant heat warm her bones. The sun is now little more than a golden hump, sinking into the river.

She has been stupid, to swim here alone at dusk. The locals have an expression word for people who do that. Shark bait.

She shivers, but not from the cold or the shock. It is the air around her. It's different. Made heavier by a gaze.

Someone is watching. Disrupting the atmosphere with their eyes.

But when she swivels to look, there is no one. Nothing there. It's like swatting at a fly.

Trinh blows her nose into her towel. Back in the breakwater, the fishing trawlers are heading out, confronting the swell as steadily as shepherds heading out to tend their flock. Later they will fan out across the horizon and string it like fairy lights.

'You late, Trinh,' her father scolds. The air in the kitchen is warm and thick with aromas of coriander, chilli, garlic, and fish sauce. Trinh's stomach growls. Swimming always makes her ravenous but she will have to wait until the dinner rush is over.

'Mama is waiting.'

Trinh clips a plastic flower behind her ear and slips on the scratchy AO Dai that Mama bought from Paddy's Market two years ago and now hangs at least three inches above her ankles.

For the customers, Dad always says. *They love that shit.*

Shit is the fourth English word he ever learned at the Villawood camp but it's his absolute favourite. He won't say what the other three were and from that, Trinh assumes they are more rude words.

Mama's welcome consists only of a raised eyebrow, which Trinh ignores by grabbing a handful of plastic menus and scurrying over to table 12 where a family of four has just settled in. Her science teacher, Mr Ellis, his wife and two little kids.

'Thanks Trinh,' he says with a friendly wink.

She likes Mr Ellis. He never gets her name wrong. Has never called her Trina. Looks her in the eye. Treats her like she's nothing different. Nothing special. He's never asked her where she comes from, not like everyone else who tends to startle when she tells them.

Cabramatta, they repeat, eyebrows rising with involuntary reflex.

At first, the whole school assumed she was a druggie. But after the first PE lesson in the pool, when she beat the boys over the fifty freestyle, the looks of wariness were replaced by something worse. Something like disdain.

In Sydney, her swimming talent made her something of a minor celebrity. Her parents were proud, even though they skulked about the pool with cat-like nervousness. But here, in this small coastal town, no one's impressed that she can swim a fifty in twenty-seven seconds flat. This town surfs. The pool's for wimps.

Mr Ellis takes the menu and orders a coke for himself, a lemon-squash for his wife, and fanta for the kids.

You know it's cheaper if you just get a jug to share, she wants to tell him.

But Mr Ellis has no need of being told that jugs of soft drink are cheaper than individual drinks and this is why he'll never truly understand. Not really.

At the end of the meal he leaves a ten dollar tip, which is pretty generous for the town and makes her feel uneasy.

'Tell your Dad he does the best

Vietnamese in town.' Mr Ellis delivers the dad-joke deadpan.

Theirs is the only Vietnamese, though there is a Chinese and an Italian, along with the two pubs, the RSL and the Maccas. All the major continents of the world covered when you think about it. Except Africa. Her Dad wanted to call it *Nguyen's* but Trinh convinced him that no one would know how to say it, so *Saigon Express* it is.

At the end of the dinner rush, Trinh and her dad take up position on milk crates out the back of the restaurant. Under the single spotlight, she gets a start on the trigonometry homework while her dad lights up a cigarette. From the kitchen come the strains of traditional Vietnamese music. Trinh's not sure if it's the crappy tape deck or if that's the way the music is supposed to sound, but the melody is scratchy and drowns out the woody calls of the currawongs. She's given up on rubbishing his music. He says it's the sound of home, but to her it is a sound that makes her feel she will never belong. Anywhere.

The morning is soft and purple as the Jacaranda petals being crushed by the wheels of Trinh's bike. The whole town is blooming with them and as she cycles up hill, she passes under pockets of purple rain where the petals are starting to fall. At the top, the water tower sits above the dumpy town like a concrete crown, but the view is 360 degrees. You see everything—the town, the river, the breakwater, the beach, the ocean and the horizon. Through the breakwater the trawlers are returning, coasting along a sea that's as flat as a sheet. If she had time, she'd go for a swim, but Mama likes her prawns straight off the boat.

Bike resting between her legs, she counts the trawlers.

Seven.

She counts again.

Still seven.

One missing. Definitely one missing.

Down the hill she pedals so fast her hair lifts behind her like a kite.

She is flying.

The marina is buzzing. Fire trucks. Police. Lights, but no sirens. Trinh dumps her bike in the dirt and hurries to the jetty. The trawler is half-submerged under water at a 45-degree angle as if caught mid-fall. The fire brigade has deployed a boom on the water to catch the petrol but the water is slick with oily rainbows.

The fishermen huddle, scratching their beards and muttering. Their prawn guy, Steven, is at the centre. Mama likes his catch the best though Trinh can't taste any difference at all. She bites down on her lip and tugs at his all-weather jacket. 'What happened?'

Steve breaks out of the circle. 'The trawler? She just came back in and sank.'

'For no reason?'

He smiles. 'There'd be a reason, Trinh.'

'Like what? A leak or a hole or something?' .

'Maybe. But I guess that's beside the point now.'

'I guess.' She wants to shake him. Make him answer. How can he just accept it like that?

'Three kilos today?'

She takes the prawns and puts them in the mini-esky that sits on the basket at the front of her bike. Her father will be fishing for flathead off the breakwall, and she'll drop them off with him. Save her the trip home.

Halfway out, she senses someone behind her, feels that weight in the air again, so she slows to get a look and let whoever it is get up beside her.

And there he is.

Casually tossing her hair, Trinh takes a good look. That guy. She's seen him before, surfing in the afternoons. He's good at it. Doesn't go to her school, she knows that, but she doesn't know if it's because he's too old, or because most of the indigenous kids just don't.

'Hey,' he says.

'Hey,' says Trinh.

'I saw you yesterday.'

'So you were the one perving.'

'Making sure you didn't die.'

She snorts. 'Like I would let that happen.'

Trinh has slowed. Her father is less than 200 metres away. She and the boy wheel about each other like birds in the sky.

'I'm doing the ocean swim on Saturday,' she says.

'Not like that you're not.'

'Why?' She stops pedalling and he stops in front of her.

'You'll die,' he says matter of factly.

Up close, his eyes are watery green. 'Meet me here this arvo.'

'Why?' In Sydney, she would have said no. But here she has nothing to lose, and the boy seems genuine.

'I'm gonna show you something,' he says. 'What's your name?'

'Trinh.'

'I'm Jed. Four o'clock. Okay?'

She nods and as he wheels away from her she has the sense of a tide, withdrawing.

In home science they make scones and Trinh is paired with Kelly McDonald who's nice enough but insists on making her own dough even though all the other pairs are working together. When the scones come out of the oven, Kelly's are perfect, golden puff balls, while Trinh's are mean and small, like bullets.

The teacher gives Kelly nine out of ten. Trinh gets a four.

'I thought your dad was a chef,' says Mrs Gallen, fingering the scone as if it may be toxic.

He's actually a lawyer. Or, he was a lawyer. Before me.

Trinh could teach Mrs Gallen how to cook a stir-fry. When Dad makes it, he tips little strips of meat into the wok which seize and shrivel and jump about in the pan, like they're trying to escape the scorching heat. When she asks him about Vietnam, he's like the meat in the wok, so she doesn't ask any more. The only time he mentions law is when he tells customers in broken English that Trinh will be leaving town next year to study law at Sydney University. In those moments, his eyes are like marbles and Trinh doesn't have the heart to tell him it's not what she wants.

'Yes, Mrs Gallen. My dad is a cook,' Trinh pauses. 'But he's not very good at it.'

Mrs Gallen smiles and changes her mark to a five.

Shoulder to shoulder, Jed and Trinh stand at the water's edge. Feet kissing the suds.

'That flat patch. Where the waves aren't breaking. That's a rip. It's the water that's been dumped on the sand, trying to get back out again fast as it can. You don't swim in that. Not unless you want an express ticket to New Zealand.' He smiles. 'That's what you swam into yesterday.'

'I meant to swim into it. I wanted to get out quick.' Trinh folds her arms.

'Well you're a bloody idiot.'

'I'm the bloody idiot that's gonna win the ocean swim.'

Jed sighs. 'You know why people drown?'

Because they get on leaky boats.

'Because they panic,' he says. 'They fight it. You've gotta go with it. Accept it. It's bigger than you.'

Trinh rolls her eyes. 'I know. I know. It's your religion, right. Spiritual and all that. You surf for the love, right?'

'Partly.' He shakes his curls and grins. 'And for the chicks.'

In the shallows they splash and porpoise through the waves. Easy. Then, Jed dives in front, goes deeper.

'C'mon,' he calls to her, the sun glistening off the golden tips of his dark curls. 'Let's get out the back.' He dips under a wave and Trinh waits for him to resurface. Five seconds. Ten. Nothing. Just an ocean full of nothing but water. No life at all. She is about to gulp at the air when suddenly he is beside her again.

'C'mon slowcoach.' He splashes Trinh and she shakes off the water.

'Do you mind if we just stay here?'

''Kay.' Splashes her again, and off he dolphins, this time towards the shallows.

Trinh exhales.

Race day is perfect. No wind. No clouds. Everything clean and pure. The swell is subdued. Obedient. Waves are rolling in, rhythmic and regular. The sand is crowded. Busy. It smells of zinc cream and rubber caps. As Trinh trudges towards the start line, she wants to be sick, or do a wee. Maybe both

The starter raises his gun.

When it sounds, Trinh bounds in with the rest of them. The water is a washing machine of legs and arms, waves and kicking. She gasps for air and finds nothing but water. Jed's words come to her.

Get to the edge. Find the clear water.

It's easier out wide. There, she can put her head down and swim like mad. Like she's taking the express ticket to New Zealand. In the water, she keeps her eyes closed and takes only an occasional look around to see that she's still on course. This way, she can almost pretend she's back in the pool. Like the black line is still there, absorbing all her thoughts so that her mind is nothing but blackness.

Another look up. Quick scan left, right. She's around the second buoy now. Headed back towards the shore, back into the impact zones where the waves are breaking. Beneath her, the water swells and surges until it has no choice but to break. When it does, it does so gently and she is carried, careful as a mother, right to the shore.

Trinh crosses the finish line, her heart large in her chest. She sinks to the ground and the sand clings to her back, thighs and legs like a second skin. Pale and golden.

At that moment, she realises the ocean is still teaming with bobbing heads. On the beach, there is almost no one else around.

Trinh curls up on the sand and closes her eyes.

She wishes Jed was by her side. She'd like to thank him, now that all the races are done. Her breath is back to normal and the thought of what is about to happen warms her from within. The loudspeaker crackles. Sun glints off the gold of the medals. She straightens her shoulders.

'Third place in the under 18 girls section.' The Surf Club president stops. Squints at his clipboard. Looks sideways, making wrinkles in the skin on his fat, sausage neck. He takes the loudhailer away from his mouth, but not quite far enough. *What kind of fucken name is this,* the loudspeaker whispers into the crowd. There are titters, and the President clears his throat.

'Third place in the under-18 girls section is Treen-a Na-joo-yen.'

Trinh shuffles through the crowd, bumping shoulders. Wanting to disappear into the sand.

A mocking voice reaches her. *Nice work, Trina-No-win.*

The Club President shakes her hand but doesn't meet her eye. She bows her head for the medal and when the cool metal touches her skin, she shivers. The applause has died before she gets back to her place in the crowd.

In the afternoon, the beach is deserted, save for the empty sunny-boys that were given out after the race. The weather has closed-in. No trawlers going out tonight. Not in this mess. But Trinh knows Jed will be here, and he is, huddled into the breakwall, barnacle-like, with his hoodie pulled down over his ears and hands jammed into boardies.

Into him, Trinh leans in. He's her shelter.

'You did it,' he says quietly.

'You were there?' She minces grains of sand between her fingers. 'What a fucking joke.'

He looks at her, silent, and nods his head towards the town. 'The shit I've been through in this place,' he breathes and shakes his head.

For a moment, they are silent, and Jed pushes off the rock.

'C'mon.' He holds out his hand and nods toward the ocean.

'You serious?'

His hand is there and Trinh takes it.

As they walk down the beach to the water, feet squeaking in the sand, she feels her mum and dad beside her. They are staring out to the horizon, and the leaky boat, and the big emptiness. Seeing what might be, if only they can be brave enough.

Near the water's edge, Jed lets go, rips off his hoodie and bolts towards the waves.

'Last one in's a rotten egg.'

Laughter bubbles up from within her as Jed leaps through the waves.

The water is at Trinh's feet now. She cups some in her hands, lets it cascade over her head. Christens herself.

I don't hate you, she whispers.

I don't hate you either, the sea whispers back.

And into the rushing white-water, Trinh dives. Head first.

Karen Andrews is an award-winning writer, author, editor, poet and publisher. Her work has appeared in journals and publications throughout Australia. She has blogged at karenandrews.com.au since 2006 and is one of the most established and popular parenting/personal bloggers in the country. She is the host of *The Creative Life* podcast, interviewing Australian writers about their creative process. Her latest book is *On The Many Shapes Bodies Will Take* and she has a forthcoming release called *Trust the Process: 101 Tips on Writing and Creativity*.

Kevin Bonnett is a Warrandyte writer and musician. He has had poetry and short stories published in a variety of Australian literary periodicals including *Overland, Muse, Blast, Famous Reporter, Vernacular* and the on-line poetry journal *Divan*. His second novel, *Soft Metal Lips* was short listed in the 2004 Varuna awards for manuscript development. The Melbourne Poets Union published his first poetry collection, *De-Icing the Wings,* in 2014. Kevin's poem *My Ashes in Central Park* was highly commended in the 2017 Melbourne Poets Union International Poetry prize. He is working on several novels including *Seven Hats*, set in gold rush Melbourne and a crime novel, *Killing Turtle*.

Avril Bradley an award-winning poet has published poetry in Australia and overseas. Her sixth collection of poetry *A needle through the camel's eye* is forthcoming from Ginninnderra Press. She was awarded an honorary degree from Roehampton University London in May 2017.

Brianna Bullen is a Deakin University PhD candidate writing a creative thesis exploring the possibilities for memory imagined in science fiction. She has had work published in journals such as *LiNQ, Aurealis, Verandah, Voiceworks, Rabbit* and *Peril*. She won the 2017 Apollo Bay short story competition and placed second in the 2017 Newcastle Short story competition. She typically writes short fiction and poetry, usually science fiction-oriented.

Laura Elvery is a writer from Brisbane. She has written for *Overland, Meanjin, The Big Issue* Fiction Edition and *Griffith Review*. She has won the Josephine Ulrick, Margaret River and Neilma Sidney short story awards. Laura is the author of the short story collection, *Trick of the Light*.

Katelin Farnsworth is a writer from the Dandenong Ranges, just outside of Melbourne, Victoria. Publications include: *Overland, Tincture Journal, Verity La, The Victorian Writer* and *Award Winning Australian Writing* 2015 and 2017. Katelin won the Rachel Funari Prize for Fiction in 2015 and came second place in the Rhonda Jankovic Literary Awards in 2017. She is represented by Hindsight Literary Agency.

Paulette Gittins began her writing career in the format she particularly loves: the short story. She has written a large body of stories and poetry, which have won local, state and national awards. Her first novel, *The Secret World of Annette Robinson*, published by HarperCollins in 2004–2005, won the NSW State Library Dobbie Award For A First Novel By A Woman Writer. A teacher for many years, Paulette's stories have also been published in two volumes of the Margaret River Press anthologies, 'Knitting and other Stories' and 'The Trouble with Flying'.

Cassie Hamer's short stories have been published by Black Inc, Margaret River Press and Mascara Literary Review. In 2017, she won the Shoalhaven Literary Award and her work has achieved success in many other awards and competitions. Her debut novel, *After the Party*, will be published in 2019 by Harlequin. Cassie lives in Sydney with her husband and three daughters. To read more of her work or to get in touch, go to CassieHamer.com.

Shelley Hansen 'Lady of Lines' is a Queenslander who has penned poetry since childhood. She has won various regional, national and international awards for her written verse and is the current Queensland Written Bush Poetry Champion. Shelley has a diverse approach to poetry, with special interest in the lesser-known stories of Australia, including her own local region. Along with husband Rod, Shelley performs at regional events, often in period costume. Shelley and Rod also regularly appeared on ABC Local Radio. She has released a book and CD of her poetry and more details can be found on her website www.shelleyhansen.com.

Of Taiwanese heritage, **Catherine Mah** is a short story writer completing a Master of Arts in Creative Writing at UTS. She lives in Sydney with her family and several half-dead houseplants.

Rachael Mead is a poet, short story writer, arts reviewer and bookseller living in South Australia. She has an Honours degree in Classical Archaeology, a Masters in Environmental Studies and a PhD in Creative Writing from the University of Adelaide. Her poetry collections include *The Flaw in the Pattern* (UWAP 2018), *The Sixth Creek* (Picaro Press 2013) and two chapbooks. You can find more of her work at www.rachaelmead.com

Jonathan O'Brien is a Brisbane-based writer, editor and creative producer. He has been described as 'a fresh and exciting voice' by *The Guardian* Australia and was awarded the State Library of Queensland Young Writers Award (2017) as well as the QUT Undergraduate Creative Writing Prize (2014). He was shortlisted for the Monash Undergraduate Prize for Creative Writing (2016) as well as the inaugural Richell Prize (2015). Jonathan is the founder of arts residency space House Conspiracy and is the editor of the 2018 arts anthology *The Conspirator*.

Mark O'Flynn's most recent novel, *The Last Days of Ava Langdon* (UQP) was short-listed for both the Miles Franklin Award and the Prime Ministers Award for Fiction. It was also the winner of the Voss Literary Award, 2017. His most recent collection of poems is *Shared Breath*, (Hope Street Press, 2017). He lives in the Blue Mountains.

Penny O'Hara is a Canberra-based poet, editor and writer. Her poems have appeared in Australian journals and anthologies including *Meanjin*, *Australian Poetry Journal*, *Cordite Poetry Review* and *Verity La*.

Fikret Pajalic came to Melbourne as a refugee and learnt English in his mid-twenties. His fiction has appeared or is forthcoming in Australia in *Meanjin*, *Overland*, *Southerly*, *Westerly*, *Etchings*, *Sleepers*, *The Big Issue* and in US journals *Hotel Amerika*, *Florida Review*, *Minnesota Review*, *Nashville Review*, *Wisconsin Review*, *Antipodes*, *Fjords Review*, *Sheepshead Review*, *Bop Dead City* and elsewhere.

Guy Salvidge is an English teacher living in rural Western Australia. The author of the dystopian novels *Yellowcake Springs* and *Yellowcake Summer*, Guy's short fiction has previously been published in *Westerly*, *Tincture Journal* and *Award Winning Australian Writing* 2016. 'The Centre Cannot Hold' won the Joe O'Sullivan Writers' Prize in 2017 and was first published in the Australian Irish Heritage Association's quarterly publication, *The Journal*. Guy is currently working on a crime novel, *City of Rubber Stamps*, and he blogs at guysalvidge.wordpress.com

Kelly Simpson lives in Melbourne with her book-obsessed daughter, partner and their very well-used library cards. Spending most of her career in the corporate sector before becoming a parent, she has always been a passionate reader and has dabbled with writing stories of her own.

Miranda Tetlow has spent more than a decade working as a presenter, producer and reporter for ABC Radio, mostly in Darwin. Her work has also featured in print and online in publications such as

Meanjin, news.com.au, *The Australian, The Sydney Morning Herald, Lonely Planet, The Canberra Times* and *The Diplomat*. In 2017, Miranda won the Northern Territory Literary Award for best short story. She also writes a blog called *Postcards from the North* (https://mirandatea.wordpress.com/) and is working on her first novel.

Roger Vickery grew up in country and coastal towns in Victoria and NSW. He now lives in Sydney. He writes poetry, short stories, plays and scripts ,which have been published/performed in Australia, Ireland, UK, India and the USA. Roger has won over 70 literary awards. Recent wins include the Bruce Dawe, W B Yeats, Ipswich, Lane Cove and Waterline Poetry Prizes. He was a finalist in the 2015 Irish Fish Poetry Award and shortlisted for the 2017 Keats-Shelley International Poetry Prize. His play, *A Nest of Skunks* (co-authored with James Balian), enjoyed a highly successful season in Sydney in 2016.

Rafael S.W. is a 27-year-old Creative Writing graduate living in Melbourne, where he writes short stories and poetry and is a founding member of Dead Poets' Fight Club. He's been published in *The Big Issue* Fiction Edition, *The Sleepers Almanac* and multiple anthologies. He is a regular contributor to *Going Down Swinging* online (http://goingdownswinging.org.au/site/tag/rafael-s-w/), recently exploring the evolution of language. He is currently

working on a few collections of short stories and a compilation of poetry and would likely get more done if he quit trying to be a chess hustler. www.rafaelsw.com

The **Ada Cambridge Biographical Prose Prize** is open to writers and poets who live, work or study in the western suburbs of Melbourne. The Young Adas were newly created in 2014 for young people aged 14 to 18 years. All prizes seek to support aspiring writers and poets of the western suburbs with a cash prize and by exposing their work to a wider audience.

The **Alan Marshall Short Story Award** is run by the Nillumbik Shire in Victoria for Australian residents, to celebrate the life and work of Alan Marshall.

The **Apollo Bay Short Story Award** is part of the Apollo Bay Writers Festival. The festival is a literary event for readers and writers in the Otway region and beyond. This year's theme was to USE YOUR WORDS.

The **City of Rockingham Short Fiction Awards** are held by the City of Rockingham Council. The 2017 award asked for stories inspired by, drawn upon or using the theme of the artwork 'Arts Centre Café' by Daniela Selir (1994).

'The Cliffy' was launched in 2015 in honour of *Warrandyte Dairy*'s founding father Cliff Green. Open to short stories between 1500 and 2000 words, the **Cliff Green Short Story Competition** is divided into two age categories 'Junior' for ages 16 and under, and 'Open' for those aged 17 and up. Winning entries receive a cash prize and will be published in the *Diary*.

Named for the founder of the organisation the **Joe O'Sullivan Writers' Prize** is held by the Australian-Irish Heritage Association, based in Subiaco, WA. Aiming to celebrate Australia's Irish heritage and the distinct culture born from it the award is open only to WA writers and asks for prose between 2000 and 4000 words.

The **June Shenfield Poetry Award** is an annual award to commemorate poet June Shenfield. The award is administered by the ACT Writers Centre in collaboration with 'Demos Journal'.

The **Katherine Susannah Prichard Poetry Competition** is for for WA-born or current WA residents over the age of 18 who have never published a full collection of poetry either in print or online. This award is sponsored by KSP-member and Poets@KSP member Flora Smith in memory of her cousin Annette Cameron, life-long friend of Katharine Susannah Prichard.

The Melbourne Poets Union was established in 1977. The **Leon Shann Melbourne Poets Union International Poetry Award** is one of several competitions they have running each year.

The **2017 NALAG Grieve Poetry Prize**, held by the Hunter Writers Centre aims to commemorate Greif Awareness Day in partnership with the NALAG Centre for Loss and Grief. Open to all Australians, the competition encourages people struggling with grief to channel their emotions into poetry.

Held by *Overland*, a radical literary magazine, the **Neilma Sidney Short Story Prize** is supported by the Malcom Robertson Foundation and named after the late Neilma Gantner. Calling for short fiction of up to 3000 words centred around the theme of 'travel' the competition is open to all writers, both nationally and internationally. The winner receives $4000 and is published in *Overland*'s first print issue for the following year.

Part of a special program at the Northern Territory Library the **Northern Territory Literary Awards** have supported both established and emerging writers from the Northern Territory for the last 35 years. The **ZipPrint Short Story Award** is for original works of short fiction up to 3000 words, with the winner receiving $1000, a NT Writers' Centre Membership and masterclass. Entries open in March and close in April each year.

Named for poet C.J. Dennis the **2017 Open Award & Marian Mayne Trophy, CJ Dennis Poetry Competition, Toolangi, Victoria** is open to writers in both Australia and New Zealand. For short stories of 500 words or poems of a maximum of 80 lines (must have rhyme and metre).

Based in Victoria the **Poetica Christi Press Annual Poetry Competition** aims to build appreciation and awareness of Christain poetry. For poems no longer than 50 lines, the competition is open to writers aged 16 years and up. Poems must be previously unpublished.

Held annually from 2006 to 2017, the **Rolf Boldrewood Literary Awards** aimed to foster the writing of prose and poetry with an Australian content. These awards honoured Rolf Boldrewood, the pen name of Thomas Browne who, during his time as police magistrate in Dubbo wrote, Robbery Under Arms, one of the first major Australian novels. The Rolf Boldrewood Literary Awards 2017 marked the final year of this competition at Macquarie Regional Library.

Supported by the Shoalhaven Arts Board and Bundanon trust, the **Shoalhaven Literary Award** is for short stories. Judged by Laurie Steed, the winner will receive a cash prize of $1500.

The **Stonnington Untitled Literary Festival Short Story Competition** is held by the Untitled Literary Festival in order to celebrate Stonnington residents and visitors. Prizes are awarded in both adult and youth categories.

Held by the Peter Cowan Writers Centre the **2017 Trudy Graham/Julie Lewis Literary Award for Prose** calls for short prose up to a maximum of 2000 words. Entries must be unpublished and not have received any previous awards or recognition.

The *Verandah* Literary Journal was launched in 1986, beneath the shade of the 'wide verandahs' of Victoria College. Established as a student-run publication, from its inception the **Verandah Genre Award** has attracted high quality work from both established and emerging writers and artists for annual publication. Each year, *Verandah* offers a number of prizes, provided by sponsors, for outstanding submissions.

The State Library of Queensland's **Young Writers Award (YWA)** is an annual short story competition for Queensland residents aged 15 to 25.